By Angelina Bell
© Copyright 2014

YOGA

The ultimate crash course to learn Yoga FAST!

Table of Contents

Chapter 1
<u>The Origins of Yoga</u>

Taking its origins from the Sanskrit word "Yuj", yoga as we know it today, is a term that literally signifies union or bonding together. In a broader context this union is a reference to connecting the individual with cosmic consciousness or the Universal Spirit.

Originating in India, thousands of years ago, the practice of yoga began evolving during the Golden Age also known as "Sat Yuga". It was a time period that demonstrated everlasting peace, plentiful blessings and when there were abounding seekers of the eternal truth. And so, based on its history and the time of its conception, yoga, even today is popularly associated with thinkers, pundits and hermits.

However, it was not until the discovery of the Indus Valley civilization that information about the origins of Yoga surfaced and became known around the world. There are a number of engravings and figures excavated that have been traced to this time period that indicate yogi practices and followings.

After the discovery of its origins, the development of yoga may be traced back to over 5,000 years ago. However, some historians believe that yoga may be a far older practice that that; going as far back as up to 10,000 years old. Yoga's long and rich history can be divided into mainly four main, but some say five, periods of innovation, practice and development.

Vedic

From one of the oldest scriptures in the world, come the ancient texts of Vedas. In Sanskrit the word Veda translates as "knowledge" and rig is interpreted as "praise". Collectively, the Rig Vedas are a collection of hymns that sing praise of a higher power. The word "yoga" first appeared in these sacred texts. The Vedas were a collection of texts comprising songs, mantras and rituals which were used by the Vedic priests.

During this time period, people practiced an established way of life where rituals, sacrifices, and ceremonies existed because they were considered a means of connection to the spirit world. Vedic yogis or rishis (mystic seekers) were called upon for illumination by the masses as these Vedic masters were believed to be blessed with a vision of the Supreme Reality.

Pre-classical

This duration in yoga's history spans a considerable period lasting approximately 2,000 years until the second century. During this time, deeply perceptive texts, known as the Upanishads surfaced. Over time as yoga slowly evolved and was developed by the Brahmans and rishis, they documented their beliefs and practices in the Upanishads. These writings, discussed in detail beliefs about the self and ultimate reality; a prime focus of which was the idea of ritual sacrifice from the Vedas.

Teachings in the Upanishads internalised this idea and stressed upon the sacrifice of the ego through self-knowledge, action /karma yoga as well as wisdom. An approximate figure of 200 texts compiles the Upanishads, one of the most remarkable being the Bhagavad-Gita, which was composed around 500 B.C.

Classical

Despite its gradual growth, yoga, in the pre classical era was still a mixed bag of different thoughts, beliefs, and approaches that more than once repudiated and countered one another.

But stepping into the classical era, yogic beliefs and practices experienced a maturity that was expressed distinctly in C.E, Patanjali's Yoga Sutras. The compilation was a collection of 195 aphorisms which depicted the first systematic presentation of yoga. It expounded the Raja Yoga where yoga is organised into an eight limbed path, all geared towards attaining Samadhi or enlightenment. Based on this creation, Patanjali is often acknowledged as the father of yoga and his sutras can be seen to have a strong influence on most styles of modern yoga.

Patanjali advocated that each individual is made of both of matter and spirit. He proposed that yoga has the capacity to restore the spirit to its absolute reality; a thought shifted the focus from non-dualism to dualism.

Postclassical

The next era of yogic development is called the post classical era in which a philosophical system known as Vedanta emerged. This period affirmed the teachings of Vedanta, which in turn is based on the teachings of the Upanishads. Vedanta advocated that there was ultimate unity in everything in the cosmos.

While during the earlier yogic eras, emphasis was solely on meditation and contemplation where the goal was to merge with the infinite; this next stage of yogic development presented a change. Instead, during this period, yogis began to investigate the hidden powers of the body. Yoga masters devised advanced yogic practices that aimed at rejuvenating the body and prolonging its life.

The focus now shifted towards embracing the physical body as a way to attain understanding and complete wisdom. Masters of this age developed Tantra Yoga with profound approaches to purge the body as well as the mind and break the barriers that bind us to our physical existence.

The scrutiny of these physical-spiritual affiliations as well as body centered practices_lead to the establishment of what is now known as Hatha Yoga, which is presently practised throughout the world.

Modern
It was not until the late 1800s or even early 1900s that yoga masters started travelling westward. Around that time, their sporadic travels and visits started gaining attention among Westerners. The first real yogic event occurred at The Parliament of Religions held in Chicago in 1893 where Swami Vivekananda, a notable yogi preacher of the day, impressed the audience and formally introduced yoga and its practices to the western world.

During the next few decades, Hatha Yoga was actively promoted by the efforts of Krishnamacharya, swami Sivananda and other yogis who practised Hatha Yoga. Of the two, Krishnamacahrya produced many notable students who would continue his legacy and add to the growing popularity of Hatha Yoga.

Swami Sivananda, on the other hand, was a prolific author who penned more than 200 works on yoga and its philosophy while also established nine ashrams and many yoga centres around the world.

It was not until 1947 that Indra Devi, an early disciple of Krishnamacharya, opened her yoga studio in Hollywood that yoga became mainstream in the west. Since then, many prominent western and Indian teachers have become pioneers popularizing Hatha yoga and gaining millions of followers. Today, Hatha Yoga has many different schools, each emphasizing the various aspects of yogic beliefs and practices.

Chapter 2

<u>What is Yoga?</u>

If you practice yoga for simple mediation, breath control, flexibility or mitigation by adopting specific bodily postures, you probably consider it a means to achieving better health and relaxation. But that is merely its perfunctory level. However, when we explore the term yoga on a deeper level, it has so much more to offer.

By definition yoga is a spiritual and ascetic discipline that among other aspects is also used for gaining health benefits and relaxation. When investigated spiritually yoga takes us into deeper levels of awareness all culminating in the effort to find answers to questions of the being, enigmas of life and contacting reality.

It is a spiritual science that not only deals with the body, breath and mind, but also ventures forward to associate with the soul, and ultimately the universe. It is a practice that is both empirical as well as theoretical.

For teaching the spiritual, yoga does not focus on what to do or what not to do but lays emphasis on how to be. It is a lesson on life where both the known and the unknown are investigated and its teachings help followers liberate themselves from the physical hardships and mental agonies of life. And the goal once again is to achieve a state of being that is free from the sadness and suffering of life as we know it.

Practitioners of yoga are propelled by the desire for self-realisation. The drive to search is prompted by the necessity of finding one self where all questions, whether physical or spiritual can be answered.

Yoga dictates that the answers all lie within ourselves. And only looking within will truly provide the much sought after knowledge.

The teachings of yoga allow practitioners a method or pathway to better understand themselves on all levels of their being. This includes the physical aspects of life, the intellectual aspect, the emotional balances, desires and actions. In addition, an individual will also understand their place in the world, and insight into how to lead a more successful life in the world.

This understanding aims to bridge the gap between the internal and external conditions of life. When practiced as a way of self-improvement, yoga teaches individuals all their hidden potential that can be used to better themselves. In the beginning the individual is probably at a stage where he or she is experiencing the everyday despairs of life. Yoga attributes this misery to a state of ignorance. Once that ignorance has been lifted and the individual is better able to see through the fog, the quality of life on all levels is sure to improve.

This amalgamation of knowledge is not meant to be taught or learnt only. Instead it is to be put into practice on a daily basis. This study of the reflective is meant for those who are confident that there is life beyond physical world of the senses and that this facet of life has nothing meaningful to behold.

The truth lies beyond the physical and this continuous transformation can only be achieved through gradual experience. There is no short cut and the progressive advancement towards self-realisation can only come about in a set of enlightened stages.

As one moves forward in yoga, an individual's ego is replaced with their spirit. Basically, what this means is that shortcomings like self-pride and self-admiration are both sidelined while qualities like self-awareness are heightened. This self-awareness allows individuals to remove any weaknesses from their life and attain a state of perfection.

In turn, this state of perfection elevates an individual to divine eminence. And because for the yogi self-awareness and not self-importance is the driving force, he will always practice the law of moderation. A yogi takes the middle path and does not overwhelm his physical senses. While yoga does not deny the physical being, it does demand spiritualisation of life.

As it has already been established, the practice of yoga is both an art and a science. And in either scenario, yogic exercises and practices are devoted to finding an equilibrium between the body, mind and spirit. The entire purpose is to aid the yogi in handling breath and body to create a consciousness of the self. When this is achieved the individual is able to live in peace, enjoy good health and be in harmony with the greater whole.

Five Principles of Yoga

To attain maximum benefits from yoga, the practice is centered on five basic principles each of which have a specific role to play in achieving optimal health, mental alacrity and heightened awareness.

Proper Relaxation:

Yoga differentiates between various aspects of relaxation such as physical, mental and spiritual. For instance, physical relaxation engages to loosen tightened muscles while releasing negative energies that may have been trapped inside the body. Mental relaxation emphasizes quieting the mind and bringing things into perspective while spiritual relaxation gears focus on the techniques of visualization and meditation in an attempt to connect the individual to the greater universe.

By releasing the tension in muscles and resting the body, an individual's nervous system is revitalized making it easier to achieve inner peace. The sense of relaxation is carried over into all aspects of life including daily activities, emotional responses, physical demands as well as perception and intuition.

The second principle revolves around the idea that the physical body is designed to move and exercise. This component of yoga encompasses the many yoga poses or asana that systematically engage different muscle groups, organs and systems of the body. Yogic poses advocate stretching of muscles and ligament, massaging internal organs, flushing toxins, while promoting flexibility of the spine, movement of the joints and improving blood circulation.

Practicing these asana frequently makes the body relaxed while simultaneously energizing and strengthening it. If certain moves prove to be too challenging for individuals, they can be modified and facilitated with the assistance of various yoga props. The key is to hold positions for a few breathing cycles to get to a deeper stretch which increases the strength, flexibility and vitality of the spine.

These asana or moves are paired with breathing techniques or pranayama that guide each move and posture so that the execution is beneficial not only to the physical but also to the mental and spiritual growth of the individual.

Proper Breathing:

Breathing techniques in yoga involve inhaling and exhaling slowly, fully and rhythmically to utilise lung capacity to their full potential. This component of yogic practice emphasizes proper breathing as it is considered a bridge between the mind and the physical body. This practice increases oxygen intake in the body while deep breaths also remove stale air from the lungs. During breathing, yogis needs to learn how to regulate the length and duration of their breaths. Breathing exercises also focus on the retention of air in the lungs as well as the pauses in between.

Proper breathing techniques in yoga can help attain a calmer and more focused mind, as well as boost energy levels for the individual.

Proper Diet:

Following a healthy dieting strategy nourishes both the mind as well as the body. Consequently it leads to mental clarity and spiritual awareness. To achieve this successfully, yogic philosophy suggests that foods eaten should be natural choices, provide well balanced nutrition and be consumed in moderation.

Food should only be consumed when hungry and there should never be any kind of over eating involved. In addition individuals are not encouraged to turn to food in times of stress, distress or anxiety. Such poor eating habits will only dull the mind and senses making it difficult to acknowledge why or how much food has been consumed. Instead, food should only be consumed for sustenance while keeping the body light and supple, the mind composed and the immune system strong.

Positive Thinking and Meditation:

Thoughts affect an individual's perspectives, conceptions and outlook on life. With a positive outlook, many of life's hardships can be overcome facilitating mindfulness and inner peace.

For this reason, yoga places importance on positive thinking to sustain mental wellbeing.it uses the techniques of meditation and relaxation to clear the mind, focus on the moment and evoke a positive attitude to enhance self-esteem. The practice of meditation also allows individuals to evaluate their own personal strengths and weaknesses letting them develop self-awareness, bring clarity and focus to mind while channeling their thoughts positively.

Chapter 3
<u>The Philosophy of Yoga</u>

Now this art of living right was accomplished many years ago in India and handed down to the rest of the world from there. Scripted in the yoga sutra of Patanjali, the text gives a detailed insight into the workings of the mind while at the same time yields an eight step plan for gaining control of the physical and meta physical elements of human nature.

The eight steps provide basic guidelines on how to live a purposeful and substantial life. Each has a holistic focus which contributes an aspect towards the completion of the individual as they move towards attaining divine eminence and every step is a recommendation for the ethical and moral conduct and self-discipline.

To take a closer look at how yoga's eight limbed path provides structure and coherence to yogic practices, here is a look at each of the eight paths:

<u>The Eight Paths of Yoga</u>

<u>Yama</u>

The first limb or yama, addresses an individual's sense of integrity and moral standards. It is a focus on how one behaves in life and handles situations. It is a reference to our attitude that we exhibit towards things and propel outside ourselves. The yamas are further sub categorised into five characteristics that are all oriented towards our place in public and how to successfully coexist with others. The five yamas are:

Ahimsa: Non violence

At a literal meaning, the word ahimsa translates as not to injure or hurt people and show compassion for all living things. On a deeper level ahimsa goes to show kindness by refraining from all violence in all situations.

Satya: Truthfulness

Satya is a commitment to truthfulness where the truth does not harm anyone. In practice Satya means being honest and truthful in our emotions, thoughts, words and deeds.

Asteya: Non stealing

Asteya is a negation of stealing. Basically this practice translates into not taking something that does not belong to us.

Brahmacharya: Abstenance

Closely used in the sense of abstinence, brahmacharya emphasises responsibility with respect to the target of moving towards the truth. It does not translate as celibacy yet at the same time it also signifies that we do not use this energy to harm anyone else.

Aparigraha: Non covetousness

This yama is significant for taking only what is necessary and nothing more. In other words, aparigraha means to not take advantage of a situation or act greedily. Taking more than what we have earned means exploiting someone else's due.

According to the yoga sutras, these five behaviors need to be a part of an individual's everyday life. Achieving these yamas gives the individual with a moral code of conduct that can help purge human nature while adding to health and happiness.

Niyama

The second limb known as niyama is a reference to self-discipline and personal observances. These rules refer to the attitude of the individual towards themselves. The niyamas are also further divided into five characteristics that provide a code for living:

Saucha: Cleanliness

This refers to cleanliness and purity. This rule has both an inner and outer aspect. By outer cleanliness, the meaning implied is keeping our self physically clean but inner cleanliness touches upon good health and a clear mind. Practicing yoga poses and breathing techniques are an essential element to achieve this state of inner cleanliness. The yoga poses or **asanas** tone and strengthen the body while breathing techniques or **pranayamas** cleanse the lungs, oxygenate blood and purify the nerves.

This internal cleanliness also refers to cleansing the mind of all negative influences like anger, hatred, greed, lust pride and delusion.

Santosa: Contentment

The second niyama is santosa or contentment. This means being at peace with what you have and not being upset or unhappy about what you do not have. Being satisfied with what you have even in times of difficulty is a growing experience for the yogi leading to a fulfilling life rather than one which is full of dissatisfaction.

Tapas: Heat; Spiritual Austerities

On a literal level the term translates as heating the body and thus cleansing it. In a broader sense it refers to the idea that we can channel our energy in a way that it helps us burn all desires which may be standing in the way of achieving a union with the Divine.

Svadhyaya: Self-study

The fourth niyama stresses self-examination. This takes into account any activity that encourages an individual to look into their person, find self-awareness and even accept one's limitations.

Isvara Pranidhana: Surrender to God

The final niyama emphasizes the celebration of the spiritual. It is an awareness that the spiritual permeates everything and through our efforts we should set apart some time each day to recognize this truth.

Asana: body postures

Asana are the body postures practiced in yoga. By practicing these positions, the yogi can hope to develop a sense of discipline and an ability to concentrate better.

This aspect of yoga is the most well-known among people especially those who turn to yoga as a form of exercise.

Yoga asanas are challenging poses that give the yogi a chance to explore and control different aspects of emotion, concentration, faith, and the unity between the physical and the celestial. With practice these asana help foster the mind and prepare the individual for meditation and self-reflection.

Pranayama: breathing techniques

Pranayama is measured, controlled breath that is very important in yoga. Breathing properly is paired with yoga postures, both working towards disciplining the body and mind. Yogis also believe the pranayama has the potential to rejuvenate the body as well as extend life. Pranayama may be practised on its own or integrated into a yoga routine.

Pratyahara: control of the senses

Pratyahara refers to sensory transcendence during which individuals make a conscious effort to withdraw awareness from the external world and outside stimuli. By conscious detachment from the senses, yogis can reflect internally. This internal reflection provides the yogi an opportunity to observe their negative habits, which may be interfering with their inner growth.

Dharana: Concentration

By now, the asana have hardened the body, the pranayama have refined the mind while the pratyahara have regulated the senses. It is now time to move towards dharana which means a state of total concentration. By having relieved themselves of outside distractions, the yogi is now ready to deal with the distractions of the mind. During concentration, which is a precursor to meditation, the yogi learns how to regulate and slow down the thought process by intently focusing on one object.

Extended periods of such concentration will then lead to meditation.

Dhyana: meditation

Meditation is an uninterrupted flow of concentration. Reaching this stage means that the mind has been completely quieted and it no longer produces thoughts. Instead, it focuses on a single flow of idea. Achieving this state produces a state of tranquility where the mind, body and intellect are silenced in the form of meditation and the yogi can then realign the inner self to the right path.

Samadhi: Union with the Divine

This is the state of enlightenment for the meditator. In Samadhi the yogi transcends the self and connects with the Divine. The completion of this yogic path is what everyone desires to aspire; peace within. This is a state that can only be achieved through practice and experienced through complete devotion.

The Six Branches of Yoga

The six branches of yoga all come with their own unique features, offering the yogi insight into different aspects of growth in an attempt to discover one's true nature. The following are those branches:

Hatha Yoga: This is the path of physical yoga and the most well known and most practiced. This type of yoga uses physical poses, or asana, pranayama and meditation to make the body healthier and more aware. The practice of Hatha Yoga aims at merging the body and the soul and fill it with life force.

Bhakti Yoga: This is also known as the yoga of devotion where the yogi sees the Divine in everyone and everything. This practice leads the individuals to love, accept and tolerate all with a heightened devotion to God. The path of bhakti is a way to have more tolerance and acceptance for everyone that the yogi comes in contact with.

Raja Yoga: This path of yoga focuses on meditation and contemplation. The word raja means royal and the focal point of this yogic branch is meditation. Raja Yoga is based on the eight limbs of yoga as mentioned previously. Through this practice, the yogi is trained gain enlightenment through self-respect. Individuals who are introspective are attracted to this type of yogic practice and often members of religious orders and other spiritual communities dedicate themselves to this type of yoga.

Jnana Yoga: This yogic path deals with wisdom and knowledge of the mind. In itself Jnana Yoga is a tribute to man's intelligence. Yogis try to surpass limitations by unifying wisdom and intellect.

This path demands development of the intellect through scrutiny of the scriptures and study of the yogic texts. Typically, those people who are intellectually inclined will turn to Jnana Yoga.

Karma Yoga: Karma Yoga is based on the belief that the present is based on the past and is a path of service. Karma Yoga requires the yogi to be selfless. This branch of yoga tries to change actions towards good, and being selfless so that it can lead to a change in one's destiny.

By being aware of this process, yogis direct all their efforts to consciously create a future that is free of negativity and self-indulgence.

Tantra Yoga: Tantra Yoga is the path of ritual or celebration. Often the most misunderstood path of yoga, this path encourages a ritualistic approach to life. However, it has come to be associated with sexuality predominantly. While sexuality is an aspect of this path, it is in spirit consecrated sexuality. In truth this path is about using rituals to experience what is sacred.

Chapter 4
<u>Benefits of Yoga</u>

Because yoga aims at the harmonious development of the body, mind and soul, its benefits also target these separate areas respectively. Practicing yoga not only delivers health benefits restricted to the physical wellbeing but also accounts for powerful results when considering mental clarity, stress reduction and even emotional prowess.

The building blocks of yoga transpire from the physical where the body becomes engaged, leading to the mental where the mind and thoughts are regulated, and finally concluding in the spiritual state. This is the order of events in which benefits will appear to the yoga practitioner and that is the order in which we will talk about what perks yoga has to offer in each state:

<u>Physical Benefits of Yoga</u>

Today yoga has evolved into a popular activity that is suitable for people of all ages, including athletes, seniors and even children. As an exercise regimen, it can be modified to suit all levels of fitness.

Flexibility:

Perhaps the most evident among physical benefits of yoga is the range of flexibility that individuals can achieve when practising different yoga poses. The vast spectrum of movement and stretching during yoga is known to improve flexibility. Over time individuals can notice a difference in how their body is able to better handle many poses that they were unable to do before. At the same time physical symptoms like pains and aches will also begin to diminish. The human body naturally loses flexibility with age that can lead to pain in some individuals and immobility in others. Also inflexibility in muscles and ligaments can also cause poor posture. Learning to do gentle yoga poses can mollify these symptoms.

Strength:
On a physical level, practices like balance and holding the breath over a period of time can all assist in building strength. Various yoga poses require individuals to do this while supporting the weight of their own body. These practices all improve strength in an individual's core, arms and legs.

The more vigorous and athletic styles of yoga like Vinyasa, Bikram and Power Yoga can all boost endurance levels in individual. These dynamic disciplines engage the whole body testing mental agility and physical stamina to keep up with the poses.

Muscle tone:
As an offshoot of improving strength, individuals can also expect to see increased muscle tone. Yoga can help shape long, lean muscles. Strong muscles can do a lot for the body. Thy not only look good but can also harbor individuals against common but painful conditions like arthritis and back pain.

Certain yoga poses can help release tightened muscles in the back, hamstrings and hips to alleviate back pain while also improving posture.

In contrast to traditional strength training where individuals lift weights to gain muscle mass, yoga offers both building muscle strength while also improving flexibility.

Balance:

As mentioned previously, yoga promotes improved balance. As we get older, we tend to lose our balance naturally and become more susceptible to falls and injurers. But for those of us who practice yoga, certain poses such as standing on one leg or headstands are effective ways of building core strength and thus improving balance.

Posture:

Poor posture can trigger many physical problems like back and neck discomfort as well as muscle and joint stiffness. Individuals with a poor posture tend to slouch forward making their necks creaks and shoulders ache. Internal organs become folded over and various muscle groups are strained. In short, it takes a lot more work for the neck and back to support your head.

Not only does poor posture look sloppy and unimpressive, it is also doing a lot of damage on the inside. Yoga poses like Child's Pose, Warrior One, Lizard Pose and Bridge Pose are just some of the positions that can help improve posture and open up and relax the middle and upper back along with the neck, chest and shoulders.

Joint health:

Many individuals who suffer from arthritis and other joint related conditions can often seek relief from pain when doing yoga. There are gentler versions of most yoga poses and individuals can choose a level that suits their needs best.

With each successive yoga session joints are taken through their full range of motion. This movement naturally assists in preventing degenerative arthritis as well as preventing cartilage from wearing out.

Pain determent:

When increased flexibility and core strength go hand in hand, the results are sure to be felt. For many individuals who suffer from different types of back pain, yoga can help alleviate some of the associated discomfort.

This is especially true for people who may be sitting for a long time, perhaps due to the nature of their job or otherwise. All that sitting down will often trigger spinal compression and tightness that can be very uncomfortable and even painful. To correct this, people have turned to yoga to help with their condition.

Certain yoga poses will also improve spinal alignment that can prevent other injuries or uncomfortable conditions.

Better breathing:

While we may not even be aware of it, most of us take shallow breaths. To address this concern, there are yoga exercises known as pranayama which are specifically devised to improve breathing practices. The focus of these exercises is to take deeper breaths that can benefit the body as a whole.

In addition, breathing exercises can also assist individuals with allergies by clearing out their nasal passages. Better breathing is also an effective way to calm the nervous system, an advantage that is beneficial on both physical and mental levels.

Improved circulation:
Many of yoga's moves and postures will get the blood flowing sufficiently. Both easy and vigorous yoga poses can achieve this as many of the relaxation exercises aid in transporting more oxygen to the cells which is a result of better circulation.

There are also twisting poses and inverted poses that can help bring fresh oxygenated blood to different body parts boosting circulation and improving energy levels.

Improved digestion:
Many of the moves in yoga target and challenge the core while others are gentle movements flowing through the entire body. This combination of gentle and intense moves have been known to balance the functionality of the digestive system. Some yoga poses can help reduce the level of stress hormones released while others can encourage insulin production. Some experts suggests doing yoga to regulate the painful and uncomfortable symptoms associated with IBS- Irritable Bowel Syndrome and indigestion.

Every individual has their own metabolic rate which is easily impacted by their lifestyle. With a more sedentary lifestyle, the metabolic rate is also slow so when an individual is introduced to yoga, this inclusion of activity in a daily routine can assist in boosting the metabolic rate as well. Better metabolism will translate into better digestive health for individuals.

Weight regulation:

Many others will turn to yoga for managing their weight fluctuations. While yoga practices are not devised for burning calories, it is true that doing yoga regularly can help individuals better understand their relationship with their body. This means that there is increased mindfulness about what is being eaten and how it will affect their body. This awareness enables individuals to make better food choices.

Another bonus offered by yoga regarding weight management is that yoga helps combat stress. A lot of people turn to food in times of stress and practicing yoga regularly can help them manage this stress and redirect their focus elsewhere.

To achieve weight loss goals, opting for the more invigorating styles of yoga like Ashtanga Yoga, Vinyaysa Yoga or Power Yoga is the sensible choice as many of these sessions can last for up to an hour and a half. Brisk movements can offer cardiovascular benefits while burning calories as well as stretching and toning muscles.

Mental Benefits of Yoga

While the physical benefits are easy to identify, the mental gains go much deeper.

Mental calmness and clarity:

Most of the yoga poses or exercises require intent concentration which can naturally have a calming effect on the mind. Moving beyond the physical, yoga will also acquaint individuals with meditation techniques that revolve around better breathing and withdrawal from everyday thoughts. In practice, these methods can be highly useful in intense situations.

Stress reduction:

With some sort of physical activity involved, the mind tends to drift away from everyday worries, concerns or hassles, and focuses more on the task at hand. As such, yoga provides a way out for the mind to disconnect from routine problems and concentrate instead on the present. This practice is also effective in calming the mind and reducing stress levels as it gives the yogi a chance to put their problems in perspective.

It is important to remember that not all problems are created equal and not all problems need identical attention. So when calming the mind, yoga can also help alleviate stress.

Uplifts moods:

With focus concentrated on the present alone, doing yoga during quiet time can help improve mood. Almost everyone is familiar with the relaxing and serene Lotus Pose that can be an epitome of composure and tranquility. Plus scientific evidence also shows that engaging in frequent yoga sessions can boost serotonin levels and release mood altering chemicals that can greatly enhance moods.

Improved focus:

A very basic factor of yoga is concentrating on the present. It has been observed that with regular practice, the mental components of coordination, reflexes, reaction times, memory can all be improved. Frequent meditation can help people recall information better since they are more used to focusing intently and less prone to be distracted by outside thoughts.

Relaxation:

Yoga advocates calmness, slowing down the breath and focusing on the present. All these techniques transfer the emphasis from the sympathetic nervous system that automatically turns to the fight or flight response to the parasympathetic nervous system that has a calming and restorative effect. A shift to the latter system lowers heart and breathing rates, reduces blood pressure as well as increases blood flow around the body. What results from all of this is called the relaxation response allowing individuals to quieten and wind down.

Better sleep:

Yoga poses provide relief in so many different ways that when it is time for the body to rest, sleep can come easily and uninterrupted to the individual. The nervous system is offered a peaceful downtime when it is time to sleep allowing it to refresh itself completely before taking on the hassles of everyday life the next day. Better sleep also translates into a refreshed mind, less fatigue, and fewer stresses.

Body awareness:

Practicing yoga regularly will offer the chance of becoming more aware of one's body. This cultivation of awareness offers a rendezvous between mind and body where the two are awakened and respond to each other. This sense of awareness creates links and unbars pathways that relax emotions while achieving inner healing.

Spiritual Benefits of Yoga

Over time yoga becomes a way of life for the yogi. It does not restrict itself to merely gaining physical benefits nor stop at achieving mental clarity. Instead it evolves into a system of self-culture. At its pinnacle, yoga disciplines the mind, the senses and the physical body. This is primarily achieved through the practice of meditation.

Meditation:

The practice of yoga when paired with meditation results in a powerful alliance. With the body at ease and the mind at peace, meditation provides a deep sense of relaxation. Spirituality attained through meditation makes managing difficult situations easier and offers balance in life. It also paves the way to achieve inner strength.

Inner strength:

Gaining inner strength is the ultimate goal of yoga where all else is defied except the Universal Truth. This also happens to be the inner most part of our being. Achieving this inner strength means that we have been successful in removing all the obstacles that previously prevented us from experiencing this state of being.

Peace and happiness:

Gaining access to inner strength only strengthens us to achieve happiness and peace. On the surface, this gives us complete control over our emotions and desires while on the inside, it empowers us to resist temptations and abandon worldly pleasures.

Increases self-esteem:

For those of us who may suffer from low self-esteem, turning to yoga can be a positive experience. Since it is essentially a mind game, gaining self-esteem involves commanding the mind. Yoga itself is centred upon the connection between the mind, body and soul, and meditation is the ideal pathway to get there. By committing themselves to self-examination individuals can start to see a different side of themselves- a better side than what they give themselves credit for. They will encounter sentiments of empathy, gratitude, forgiveness and self-worth and when coming closer to the truth will begin to value themselves more.

In addition, becoming more aware of their body and state of mind can help individuals improve their relationships with others around them. As yogis learn to relax, breathe and nourish themselves, they also capacitate themselves to take better care of others around them

Search for truth:

Attaining spiritual benefits for each yogi is a personal inner journey. It defines a relationship with one that is beyond us as individuals. The relationship is a culmination with something greater than us or one that was a source of life. From the yogic viewpoint, this spiritual truth is cultivated by sharpening our awareness and nourishing self-development. In a nutshell, yoga culminates in harboring and polishing all physical, mental and spiritual development alongside each other.

Frequent yoga practice is the commencing point towards this awareness and many yogis feel this connection between their body, mind and spirit after doing yoga for a continuous period of time. Eventually, this feeling of unity achieved through movement, meditation and breathing techniques can successfully calm the confusions of the mind and fluctuating thoughts and enhanced awareness brings a greater understanding of the purpose of this world and leads to spiritual fulfilment.

Chapter 5
<u>How to Get You Started</u>

Making up your mind on doing yoga is the first step. In fact, nothing could be easier! But now that you have decided on taking up this practice, it is time to get some general information about yoga and how to make it into a successful venture.

For starters, it is important to know that there are different yoga types and that not every single type may be suitable for everyone. On the contrary there are yoga sessions that are targeted to general health as well as those that look after the needs of specific conditions.

For instance yoga can be practiced to address health concerns like arthritis, can be done to relieve discomfort during pregnancy and facilitate delivery, and may be carried out for stress relief and even for weight loss. So it becomes important to pick one type that complements not only your personality but also the level of your physical fitness.

<u>Types of Yoga</u>

To decide which type of yoga may be most suitable and beneficial for you, here is a look at some different types of yoga styles. This is also an opportunity to get familiar with the names as they will keep appearing in later parts of the book. While some of these yoga styles will recur in greater detail in future chapters, others just need a quick mention here:

Ashtanga Yoga:

Ashtanga yoga comprises an established and strenuous sequence of poses that move rapidly transitioning from one posture to the next each paired with a timely inhale or exhale. Moves in an Ashtanga yoga session will vary between standing, seated, inversions and backbends before the final relaxation.

This type of yoga is often recommended for people who want to lose weight, may enjoy indulging in a demanding workout series or wish to develop flexibility and endurance. Because there is an arrangement of poses to follow, participants need to know the sequence before they join.

Bikram Yoga:

This type of yoga is performed in a heated room rather like a sauna like environment. Temperatures may be cranked up to around 105 degrees Fahrenheit.

Once again this yoga style is considered favorable for weight loss and booting stamina. Just tolerating the heat itself is an endurance test for participants.

Hatha Yoga:

One of the original branches of yoga, hatha yoga is a physical yoga practice. Initially it was practiced to prepare the body for meditation and is a generic term that is used to refer to any type of yoga that teaches physical postures. Focus is on slow and gentle movements that can ideally suit new comers to yoga.

Hatha yoga students will practice slow paced stretching moves accompanied by simple breathing exercises and some sort of seated meditation.

This type of yoga is practiced for calming down, de-stressing and unwinding.

Iyengar Yoga:

Iyengar yoga uses props like blocks, straps, blankets and incline boards to facilitate getting into position with a keen focus on precise alignment and deliberate sequencing. With this type of yoga students learn that there is a right way to conduct each posture that will lead to perfect balance.

Kundalini Yoga:

A fairly recent type of yoga style, Kundalini yoga incorporates constantly moving, invigorating poses making the moves appear fluid. For this yoga style, participants need to know the seven **chakras** or spots where energy will be directed to flow.

Each pose in this series is carried out with a specific breathing technique that attempts at releasing energy in the lower part of the body and permitting it to move upwards. Kundalini sequences are called **kriyas** and comprise of quick, repetitive movements coordinated with deep breaths.

Power Yoga:

This is an athletic and active style of yoga that has been adapted from traditional Ashtanga tradition. Its approach is a fitness based one loosely established on the Ashtanga model.

This type of yoga is a good option for people who want a cardio like work out while also working on other aspects like endurance and flexibility. Ideally participants should be quite fit and enjoy working out. But if they are looking for chanting or meditation, they should look elsewhere.

Prenatal Yoga:
This yoga style practices poses that have carefully been adapted for expectant mothers. This yoga style is beneficial to women in all stages of pregnancy and can even yield benefits in getting back in shape after the baby arrives.

It offers a safe method of exercise during pregnancy and wards off aches and pains during this time.

Restorative Yoga:
Restorative yoga is a relaxing kind of yoga that practices gentle postures using yoga props. It is a practice which can be a good complement to more active type of workouts. Poses are held for extended periods often spanning up to 15 or even 20 minutes. With the extended duration participants will likely feel the stretch even though they may be well bolstered and supported by props.

Vinyasa yoga:
Known as flow yoga, Vinyasa Yoga demonstrates fluid movements that are synchronized with breaths in between. There is a lot of variety in this type of yoga and both Ashtanga Yoga and Power Yoga can be classified under this broader umbrella.

Getting Started

To get you started here are a few recommendations to make the task easier and yoga more enjoyable:

Pick a yoga type to suit your style:

For most beginners, Hatha Yoga is generally recommended. Being one of the most often used types, Hatha Yoga uses gentle movements and basic postures. Suitable for newcomers or those who are unable to follow a more intense exercise regimen Hatha Yoga offers slow paced stretching activities accompanied by simple breathing exercises. Classes may also include some seated meditation.

Another reason why Hatha Yoga comes so highly recommended is because it is a good starting point to become familiar with many of yoga's beginner poses, relaxation techniques, as well as with the practice itself.

Hatha Yoga offers a relaxed environment and serene feeling to its participants where it is carried out in a slow and meditative setting. However, Hatha Yoga but may not be for everyone. If you feel that you need to incorporate a somewhat more invigorating routine into your day, then you can consider another good starting point in Vinyasa Yoga.

Vinyasa Yoga on the other hand, synchronizes movement and breath together and is aptly known as flow yoga. In this type of yoga, there is a smooth flow between the different poses where one pose cascades into the next and gives the semblance of dance like movements. The breath component in Vinyasa Yoga is important as the shift from one pose to the next is guided by an inhale or exhale.

Very different from Hatha Yoga, Vinyasa Yoga allows for plenty of variety which uses movement, stretching, chanting and this diversity is its strength.

Both types of yoga offer good starting points for beginners and once you feel you have mastered the movements, you can always move on to something more advanced later.

Familiarize yourself with beginner's yoga poses:
Because there are so many, yoga poses can be overwhelming for new students. Simply start with the very basics and as you progress through each stage, the names and positions of the **asanas** will become familiar territory. With each successive session, students will start to feel more comfortable and intimate with poses, but here are a few basic ones that are appropriate for beginners:

Standing poses: These types of poses are often the most exhausting for new students. These are introduced earlier in the sessions to teach a sense of being grounded to the floor promoting alignment and posture among other factors. Some common standing poses include Downward Facing Dog, Extended Side Angle, Garland Pose and Half Forward Bend.

Balancing poses: Doing balancing poses for beginners help strengthen the core which is a prerequisite for many advanced yoga poses. Though challenging for many newcomers, the Plank Pose, Tree Pose and Side Plank variations are taught at the beginner level.

Backbends: Definitely not the easiest of postures, backbends are important for spinal health. Beginner's versions will include gentle flexing and extension of the spine that can be taught by doing the Bridge Pose, Cobra Pose and the Cat-Cow Stretch.

Seated poses: Typically used for meditation, seated poses for beginners are often practiced at the end of a session. The purpose is to stretch the warmed up body and let the cool down begin. Some of the basic versions include the Cobbler's Pose, Knee to Head Pose, Seated Forward Pose and the Staff Pose.

Pranayama: These ate breathing techniques that teach control, balance and concentration. Pranayama will be naturally incorporated in all different yoga poses. Typically, inhalations are usually paired with upward or expanding movements such as raising the arms or going into a backbend. Exhalations, on the other hand work with downward or contracting movements, such as lowering the arms or going into a forward bend.

Find a class nearby:
Getting started can be from the comfort of your own home or you can just as easily join a class with other fellow yogis. It all depends on the comfort level of individuals. Some people may prefer to practice yoga on their own while others feel that they will benefit more when doing yoga with others.

Of course, nothing beats practicing yoga with the professional assistance of a trained teacher. For a first time student such expert advice will go a long way, but if circumstances do not allow it, yoga can be done at home with the assistance of a good DVD series or program. There are also many books available to get started but it is harder to read instructions than follow a DVD where visual instruction can simply be copied.

DVDs are designed with individual needs in mind and can provide sessions that teach a range of standing and seated poses. Moreover, considerations like early morning yoga which is generally gentle, as opposed to a more vigorous routine can also be purchased separately.

If you decide to work out at home, choose a spot that is away from distractions. Ideally it should be a place that is quiet, clean and well ventilated.

When finding a class to join, it is recommended to locate one near home so that travel time is short and you feel fresh when arriving to class. Do not let factors like travel time wear you out before you even reach the class.

To look for a class, there are various online resources that can help locate yoga studios in the vicinity. Or else, other resources can include wellness magazines or local newspapers. On occasion, gyms may also offer yoga classes; just be sure to find one that has a beginner level.

What to bring to a yoga class:

The great thing about yoga is that it can be done anywhere, anytime and with the least of accessories. There is not much to bring except a yoga mat and the dress code is loose comfortable clothing.

Traditionally, yoga is practiced barefoot but individuals may wear socks or soft shoes if they wish.

Yogis will tell you, however, that beginners need to come with an open mind and a great attitude.

What to expect in the first class:

In a class setting, students will place their mats facing the teacher at the front of the studio. When finding a spot to put down your mat remember to place it at a little distance from your neighbor's so that everyone has ample space while doing poses and different movements.

Students will typically be sitting in a cross legged position or **Sukhasana** waiting for the class to commence. The first few moves will involve some gentle stretches to get into the mood and the instructor may even start things off by some chanting. Some yoga instructors may like to add in some breathing exercises or **Pranayamas** at the start of class while others may start with some meditation.

As the class progresses, there will be installments of warm up poses, yoga poses, some stretches and winding down with **Savasana** or final relaxation. All yoga sessions conclude with this pose as it is a resting position which allows the body some time to process the information received during the session.

Time and duration of a yoga session:

When practicing at home, a good time to include a yoga session in the day is early morning. This will revitalize the mind and rejuvenate the body. On the other hand, gentle practices like breathing and meditation can soothe the mind and body before a good night's sleep.

For beginners yoga sessions need not be prolonged and can range from 15 minutes to 30 minutes in duration. Intensity should be at a level where no pain is felt and just like in regular exercise the progressive order of movements should be from easy poses to the more difficult ones. It is important to relax between exercises so as not to cause fatigue.

What not to do before a yoga class:

Since it is going to be an exercise session of sorts, it is recommended to not have a big meal just before class. Instead opt for a light meal or even snack a couple of hours before the class is scheduled to start. This is good advice especially since many of the yoga poses require twisting, leaning and bending forward and sideways.

On a full stomach, all this movement can easily result in discomfort and nausea.

Keeping well hydrated on the other hand, is highly recommended. It is advised to drink water sometime before and definitely after class. For some advanced types of yoga that may result in excessive sweating, such as Bikram Yoga, participants will often take water containers with   them   to   class.

Chapter 6
<u>Yoga Equipment for Beginners</u>

The practice of yoga is all about connecting the mind and body. Its intrinsic application does not really demand any equipment at all, for yoga can be done simply sitting and breathing mindfully. That being said, there are some yoga items and equipment that can come in handy for specific poses. Using this equipment can make these poses more comfortable and easy to practice.

This is especially true for beginners who might be at a stage where their flexibility and balance still need work and certain yoga positions may appear intimidating. To develop core strength and flexibility using these items can help the individual feel more at ease and enable them to hold the positions longer.

Clothing

Choosing the right attire for a yoga session can make the difference between comfort and discomfort. And so, to get the most out of their range of motion, yoga students are always advised to wear comfortable clothing. Today's fast growing yoga clothing industry offers many styles and price ranges to choose from. Individuals can opt for one that suits their style and offers functionality at the same time.

Opting for breathable stretchy clothes is a good starting point. Since many of the yoga poses require bending where the head comes below the hips, it is a good recommendation to choose a somewhat form fitting shirt so that it does not slide down.

Wearing a very loose shirt will likely slide with the move. For bottoms, any style of exercise pants can work fine although super slick lycra type pants should be avoided as they may cause individuals to slip in certain yoga poses.

While clothing styles for women will typically concentrate on full length pants or leggings for yoga, there are also some mid length capri style bottoms available as well. For men, on the other hand, yoga bottoms can range from full length pants to yoga shorts as well.

At times the clothing style for yoga will also be dictated by the type of yoga the individual wants to practice. For instance, yogis who do Bikram Yoga will naturally prefer to opt for shorts than full length pants as the moves can be rather sweaty.

Apparel for Hot Yoga Classes

Yoga apparel for a specific type of yoga known as Hot Yoga is going to be quite different from the traditional types of yoga. Here participants take part in yoga sessions that are carried out in a heated room where temperatures are maintained at 95-100 degrees Fahrenheit. It is a style of Vinyasa practice where working in a heated environment promotes profuse sweating and raise body temperature.

Experts advise that choosing form fitted capris for women are the best type of bottoms to wear as shorts may make legs too slippery and present a hazard in balancing poses like the Crow Pose. For men the best type of shorts should fit close to the body and be made of good wicking fabrics.

Once again a close fitting tank top or sports bra is recommended for female students attending a Hot Yoga class while men have the option of going shirtless.

Footwear:

As mentioned previously, yoga is performed barefoot which makes balancing moves so much easier to carry out. Going barefoot also serves the dual purpose of providing underfoot traction to prevent slipping while also giving the feet an opportunity to exercise their full range of motion.

Yoga mat:

Since many of the positions to be practiced during a yoga class will take place sitting on the floor, a yoga mat is the most essential item that a yogi needs. Even when not in a seated position, poses that demand lying down, standing, bending forward or twisting and stretching will also require feet, knees or the back to balance and place itself of the floor.

Also known as a sticky mat the yoga mat also helps define personal space for individuals. As a safety feature, yoga mats create traction for better balancing and grip so that individuals are less likely to slip as the workout gets harder and conditions get sweaty. There is added padding and resistance underneath to prevent the hazard of injuries.

When thinking of purchasing a yoga mat, beginners need to keep a few key considerations in mind. For instance, it is important to ensure that the mat is long enough. This will guarantee that when you go down in poses like Downward Dog, your hand as and feet are both on the mat. Additionally, think about the thickness of the mat you intend to purchase. This can be dictated by the location of your yoga sessions; if practicing at home on a carpeted surface, the mat need not be extra thick for even a thin one will suffice.

But if yoga classes are to be conducted in a gym or studio on a hard floor surface, then a thicker mat will serve better.

At the same time, the type of yoga in session will also demand a specific type of mat; a more vigorous class like Vinyasa Yoga, Ashtanga Yoga or Power Yoga will need a denser mat than a light one so that you do not get bruised while working out. A gentle yoga session, on the other hand can work with a lighter mat.

As a buffer, yoga mats cater additional cushioning on an otherwise hard surface. And a good quality yoga mat will keep yoga learners comfortable and safe.

Other Yoga Props

Restorative yoga is a type of relaxing yoga which uses a number of different props. These supporting items are used to assist the body in holding poses for prolonged periods and usually involve a number of passive stretching moves. Most of these postures are adapted from seated yoga positions where aids like yoga blocks, bolsters, and blankets are used to prevent unnecessary straining.

Yoga block

Another helpful tool for beginners, a yoga block helps individuals get into certain yoga poses and maintain good posture when it is a little challenging to reach the floor without any assistance. Yoga blocks can provide assistance in an assortment of yoga poses and can be a suitable prop for all levels. These are available in wood as well as foam variations.

Typically blocks are used to function as a hand or foot rest when the yogi is unable to reach the floor during a certain position such as the Half Moon pose. Additionally, yoga blocks may also be used for providing support to the back or other limbs.

Yoga blocks are available in different heights to suit individual needs and come in a lightweight construction for easy handling. When using foam blocks, they should also be dense enough to support the full weight of the yogi. Using yoga blocks properly can assist with both flexibility and alignment.

Yoga bolster

While yoga blocks are typically made of wood of foam, yoga bolsters are long pillows that help support the body and assist individuals to relax in certain poses. They can be a very suitable prop for beginners as using them can help hold difficult positions longer while making it somewhat more comfortable to hold the pose. Getting this additional support from yoga bolsters can assist individuals relax and stretch while focusing on their breath in positions where they need to support the body.

A yoga bolster will serve many functions including supporting body weight without additional exertion. Since it helps the yogi get in a more comfortable and relaxing position, the body is then better able to be receptive while focusing on the yoga pose. Its comfortable support underneath the back, neck or hips allows tightened muscles to release gradually and gently. And its use is manifold to find support in poses like supported Child's Pose, supported Twist, Easy Reclined Heart Opener as well as supported Upward Dog and supported Downward Dog among many others.

Yoga bolsters are used extensively in restorative and prenatal yoga classes.

Yoga belt or yoga strap

Yoga belts or straps are used to assist practicing yogis get into position while they are still improving their flexibility. They can be highly effective during positions where the arms are not long enough or the body not open enough to reach feet or other body parts. In positions where there is a need to go deeper into the pose, a yoga belt or strap can help provide the additional support.

While a sturdy rope or scarf can also serve the same purpose, yoga belts or straps are designed with a buckle or loop to assist users in creating a loop for the hand or foot when holding a pose. Using yoga belts not only help support and align the back but also when extending the grasp. Belts are particularly effective in stretching muscle groups especially the hamstrings.

When use appropriately, yoga belts or straps are useful tools for yogis of all levels. As mentioned earlier, rope usage not only enhances flexibility but also aims to correct alignment while functioning as a modifier for people who may suffer from back or shoulder injuries. A typical yoga strap can range from being about 6 to 9 feet long with a loop enclosure to assist in altering the length. Most belts will be made from thick cotton or hemp material.

Yoga belts can come in handy when positioning oneself in poses like the Cobbler's Pose, Standing Hand to Big Toe Pose, Reclining Leg Stretch and the Cow Pose among others.

Yoga blanket

Yoga blankets are used as props to lie down on or sit on during the class.

They can be placed on the floor to cushion the back during reclining positions and can also be used as a wrap during the final Relaxation Pose at the end of the yoga session.

For beginners, folded yoga blankets may be placed under the hips to elevate them above the knees for a better and more comfortable seated position.

Sitting up tall on a yoga blanket can give the spine some extra lift and the hips more room to relax. Additionally, it can also make moves like Crescent Warrior more endurable by taking pressure off the joints and permitting the yogi to focus more on holding the position more comfortably. The Pigeon Pose is another seated position where using a yoga blanket by rolling it up and threading it under the bent leg can deliver additional support and comfort.

Yoga blankets can also provide supplementary cushioning when doing more advanced positions like the Shoulder Stand by providing support under the shoulders and protecting the neck.

Yoga towel

Depending on the type of yoga practiced, the end result may be a sweaty one. Here yoga towels are a must for the most advanced and vigorous types of yoga such as Bikram Yoga, Power Yoga or other types of Hot Yoga.

Too much sweat can make the mat slippery and consequently dangerous, so there may be a need to cover it up with an absorbent towel. While a standard towel can also work, it should cover the mat underneath completely to avoid slips and falls. Plus, there are specially designed yoga towels that come with rubber nubs on the underside to prevent unnecessary slipping.

These yoga mat towels are also designed to be extra absorbent so that they are not only a handy tool for drying off sweat during a hard workout but also serve the dual purpose of offering support in certain yoga positions.

Yoga bag

For those who practice yoga at home, this is not a must have accessory but others who have joined a class may want to carry their yoga mat in a bag. Specially designed to hold yoga mats, yoga mat bags are handy in keeping the mat rolled up and compact making it easy to handle.

Yoga bags are also available in a variety of sizes so that they can store not only the yoga mat but may also have different pockets and chambers to fit other yoga accessories like yoga belts, blankets or towels. Some designs may also feature smaller compartments to hold phones and wallets as well.

Chapter 7
<u>Yoga Poses</u>

Just as there are so many benefits that practicing yoga offers, there are an equal number of poses that reap those benefits. These poses or positions are known as asana each of which offers definitive physical and mental benefits. And while it is very difficult to look at each and every yoga pose that there is, a simpler way of cataloging them can be according to the pose type.

For instance, it is clear by now that although there are different types of yoga, both gentle and vigorous variations, they all use the same basic moves and vary their intensity to suit individual needs. It is important for the yogi to recognise their body's abilities and limitations before beginning their asana. New students should never force the body into a pose or try and go beyond their limit. And even though progress may be slow initially, given time the body will become more flexible.

At the start, beginner's poses aim to build basic strength and flexibility for the whole body. Here students get to work with a combination of standing, seated and supine stretches while also getting into some basic backbends and balancing poses. At this point students should ease themselves into each position and check to see if there is any tension while holding that position.

At the intermediate stage, yoga poses begin to demand a greater demonstration of strength, balance and flexibility. Some new additions at this stage will be the introduction of arm balances and inversions into the workout while the existing difficulty level of standing poses and backbends will be increased.

For advanced yogis, yoga poses will progress into deeper moves requiring a great deal of both strength as well as flexibility. Such stamina and resilience comes to advanced yoga practitioners through years of practicing the poses repeatedly.

Here we will look at yoga poses by type ranging from arm balances, backbends and chest openers to hip openers and inversions, to seated poses and twists, preferably in alphabetical order to make it easy to follow.

Arm Balances: By no means a move for novice yogis, arm balances only rank as the first type of pose on this list as it is the first in alphabetical order. And although arm balancing moves themselves are highly challenging, there are a number of easier versions that can prepare new yoga students to build up their arm strength.

Among these are the Plank Pose, the Side Plank or the Downward Dog Pose which are moderate poses to start with. Both poses require putting weight on the arms while at the same time testing abdominal strength. Once these poses have been mastered, students can actually attempt lifting their feet off the floor (balancing solely on the arms) and move on to more advanced moves like the Crow Pose with variations such as the Half Crow or the Lifted Half Crow Pose, the Crane Pose, Firefly Pose, Peacock Pose and the Scale Pose among the more challenging moves.

Arm balances provide opportunities for the yogi to develop strength, body awareness as well as focus. Arm balances will only be performed successfully once the yogi has attained a certain amount of upper body and torso strength to carry out and hold the position for a certain period of time.

But upper body strength is not the only requisite for doing arm balances. These moves also require a fair amount of flexibility especially in the spine for many of the moves also involve rounding forward and twisting in motion. Being flexible allows certain areas of the body such as the neck for instance, to be relaxed while holding a pose.

Backbends: Incorporated in many beginner's yoga sequences, backbends open up and lengthen the front of the body. These moves demand a deep spinal extension as opposed to the forward bend where the back of the body is lengthened instead. In addition to improved spinal alignment and movement, backbends also strengthen back muscles, increase the range of motion in the shoulder and hip joints and release tension in the shoulders and neck.

Some of the beginner level backbends include the Bridge Pose, the Chair Pose, the Crab Pose, the Extended Dog Pose and the Warrior 1 pose.

Broadly speaking, backbends can be categorized into three types where the first type involves traction. In these positions the body bends with gravity engaging the muscles at the front of the body in poses such as the Camel Pose or the Upward Bow Pose.

The second type of backbends work with leverage where the strength of the arms and legs are tested to deepen the move. These include poses like the Cobra Pose and the Bow Pose.

The third type of move classified under backbends contract muscles on the back to counter gravity. These moves typically involve lying on the front and bending such as in the Locust Pose.

Balance poses: Doing balance poses in yoga requires a combination of strength and relaxation simultaneously to exhibit perfect balance.

These types of poses also demand the most concentration on the yogi's part when compared to other types of poses and are beneficial in developing core strength, improving coordination, posture, confidence and even memory.

Well known balancing poses include the Eagle Pose, Extended Head to Big Toe Pose, Half Moon Pose, Side Plank Pose, Lord of the Dance Pose and the Tree Pose to name just a few.

Balance poses are so varied in yoga because they provide a combination of balance both in the body as well as the mind. Each pose works to strengthen different muscles and joints. For instance, standing balance poses target the legs and knee joints, whereas arm balances reinforce strength in the arms, shoulders and wrists.

On the emotional front, balance poses are useful for stress relief, relieving fatigue and decreasing tension. Because these poses require focused attention on so many levels, practicing the poses takes the mind off of everyday worries and re-channels them into concentration and attention.

Core yoga poses: A strong core grants individuals greater strength and improved stability. Yoga poses that focus on core strength improve posture, tone muscles, strengthen the spine and improve the chance of preventing injury. Through these poses an individual can hope to overcome numerous physical limitations.

By doing all this core strength moves in yoga help keep the yogi steady in all types of asana; it stations the spine upright is standing positions, grants flexibility in backbends and permits individuals to maintain and sustain balance. Without a strong core, all moves are in danger of disintegrating and leading to injury.

Beginner core moves include postures like Balancing Table, Crab Pose, Half Bow Pose, Four Limbed Staff Pose, One Leg Boat and the Shiva Twist pose.

Forward bends: Forward bends can be done in both standing and seated positions. These moves create length and space in the spine, will counteract compression and activate abdominal muscles. Forward bends open up the back, assist in complete exhalation of air from the lungs and are beneficial for calming the mind.

Basic moves include the Big Toe Pose, the Bound Angle Pose, Child's Pose, Extended Puppy Pose and the Standing Half Forward Bend.

When doing a forward bend in yoga, it is important to keep alignment in mind. Experts advise students to lengthen the front of the body during the fold, while keeping a relaxed neck and jaw. If the move is too challenging, then simply bend the legs slightly at the knees to better balance.

Individuals can also choose to make good use of yoga props in many of these moves. Standing forward bends can be facilitated by working with yoga blocks while seated forward bends can be made more comfortable by using yoga blankets, toga straps and yoga towels. Props can also assist in preventing the back from over rounding and injury.

Hip openers: For most people who sit for long periods, the hips tend to become tight causing pain and soreness in the hip, sometimes extending into the lower back. The same can happen to people who engage in sports like running or cycling. While many yoga postures involve the muscles around the hips, hip openers are a definitive set of moves that target this area and aim at developing a heathy range of motion in the hips.

With this series of moves, students of yoga can hope to alleviate back pain, achieve a standing pose they might have been struggling with and improve circulation in the legs.

When doing hip opening exercises in yoga, the joints and muscles in the area are opened up. The moves assist in keeping the hips as well as the pelvis in good alignment and can prevent strain and tightness while increasing the range of motion in the area.

These poses may be practiced in standing, seated or supine positions. There are specifically four area that hip openers will aim to target such as quads and hip flexors through moves like Lunges, Bridges and Saddle Pose. To work on the hamstrings, yoga poses like Downward Facing Dog and Half Butterfly Pose are recommended.

Yoga asana focusing on the groin and adductors include poses like the Happy Baby Pose, Butterfly Pose and wide legged forward bends like Wide Angled Seated Forward Bend Pose. And finally, yoga asana for working on the glutes and IT band include The Cow pose, Easy Pose or Lotus Pose.

Other ideal poses for beginners include the Child Pose, Warrior Pose and the Triangle Pose. Once comfortable with these poses, students can then progress to more challenging yoga poses like the Eagle Pose, Half Moon Pose, Lotus and the Pigeon Pose.

Inversions: As the name implies, inversions are positions where the head is at the ground level with the legs and feet elevated higher. These poses can be fun yet challenging but are a sure way to improve circulation. Placing the body in this unusual configuration, where the heart is higher than the head helps deliver fresh supplies of oxygenated blood to the brain. These positions also help the yogi improver balance, stability as well as strength.

According to yogic philosophy, it is believed that many of the impurities in the body are stationed in the lower part of the abdomen. When the individual practices an inverted position, it allows these impurities to move in the opposite direction, permitting them to travel from the lower abdomen into the digestive tract where they can be burnt off. This will then enable the yogi to breathe deeper and improve their overall health.

Additionally, inversions alter the flow of the cerebral spinal fluid, permit blood to drain from the lower body replacing it with fresh blood to circulate around the different organs and generally reverse the action of gravity on the body; instead of pulling everything towards the feet, the orientation shifts towards the head.

When thinking if inversions, poses like Headstand, Shoulder Stand and Forearm Stand immediately come to mind, but there are simpler as well as gentler variations for beginners. Even postures like Downward Dog, Standing Forward Bend, Legs up the Wall, and Happy Baby Pose are all placid inversions in yoga.

Restorative yoga poses: Just as yoga can be an active practice, it also has a softer side to it. Like supine poses, restorative poses in yoga offer the yogi a chance to relax, heal and restore. These pose prepare the body and mind for meditation and relaxation while taking the students into a deep state of mitigation. By relaxing, restorative poses help individuals improve their concentration, and stimulate the mind. These poses are made more effective by using a number of yoga props such as blankets, bolsters, straps that can help deepen the practice or be used as aids in postures that require a higher degree of flexibility.

Practicing restorative yoga moves can be very handy when trying to eliminate fatigue and weariness caused by daily activities. In addition restorative yoga can also help individuals recover from physical injuries, illnesses and overcome emotional depression and traumatic despair.

Often many of the restorative poses will overlap or coincide supine poses like Legs up the Wall, Reclining Big Toe Pose, Child's Pose, Reclining Bound Angle Pose and the Corpse Pose.

Seated yoga poses: Because a lot of our time is spent sitting down with poor posture, seated yoga poses can help re-train the spine to become stronger, straighter and suppler. These poses include a broad range of positions that can benefit the spine by stretching it straight, along with the muscles in the back. Seated poses also release muscular tension in the back and a well-rounded practice of seated asana will improve alignment and flexibility for the practicing individual.

With many of the seated positions, there is forward or backward bending involved along with some twisting as well. When done properly, these moves can correct structural defects of the spine. In addition, seated poses and their corresponding movements massage internal organs while correcting alignment as a result of which organs are able to function properly.

Seated asana not only strengthen the back muscles, they also reinforce the core, upper thighs and obliques. Additionally, seated asana help clear tension from the body, stimulate internal organs and calm the mind. That is why meditation is performed in a seated position. Breathing and meditation exercises done in a seated position can help calm down both the mind and the body.

Most seated yoga poses are appropriate for beginner students and many of these can be conveniently adapted to suit any level of flexibility and strength. Beginner level seated poses include the Boat Pose, the Fire Log Pose, the Half Lord of the Fishes Pose and the Seated Forward Bend.

Standing poses: Standing poses from an integral part of any yoga class as they are basic grounding and centering moves. On a physical level, these poses emphasise balance, resilience, strength, as well as stamina. Standing poses in yoga focus on all these features concurrently and take the body through a full range of motion. Once the yogi has found his balancing point he can then realign his body comfortably.

Many of these energetic poses are classified as equilibrium poses and aim at regaining balance both in the body as well as in the mind.

Standing sequences can include yoga poses like the Triangle, Side Angle, Basic Standing Forward Bend and the Tree Pose among others.

Supine yoga poses: These types of poses are done lying on the back and are a good way to end any yoga session. Supine poses are helpful in releasing stress, promoting flexibility and allow a full range of motion while using the ground or floor as a supporting prop.

Most of these reclining positions calm the mind and nervous system, rejuvenate the body, can stretch and relax the lower back as well as assist in relieving fatigue. Among these the Corpse Pose often concludes the yoga session. Another called the Reclining Big Toe Pose, targets the legs, as well as the pelvic region while giving a deep stretch to the calves, thighs and hamstrings.

Beginner level supine poses include the Corpse Pose, the Fish Pose, Belly Twist, the Bridge Pose and Half Supine Hero Pose.

Twists: Twisting moves in yoga are an effective way to flush out toxins from the body and stimulate the circulation. By careful yet gentle twisting movements, the yoga student will promote blood flow in the midsection while also massaging internal organs.

There are a number of level appropriate twists for student to work on and progress as they master the moves. Practising twisting poses will improve a yogi's overall performance making once challenging poses easier to do and more accessible to practice.

Twists in yoga involve a strong rotation in the torso as the chest is opened and expanded. The moves compress internal organs upon twisting and when the pressure is released, a flow of oxygenated blood circulates back into the organs triggering a cleansing effect.

Twists are a standard yoga move in most classes ranging in difficulty from easy to advanced. For beginners simple twists can include moves like Half Lord of the Fish Pose, Mariachi Pose, Revolves Triangle Pose and the Revolved Side Angle Pose.

Chapter 8
<u>Yoga Poses for Stress Relief</u>

Practicing yoga on a frequent basis has shown proven benefits for reducing stress, staying in shape as well as calming the mind. However, when it comes to doing yoga for stress relief, there are certain poses that are especially instrumental in prompting relaxation, relieving tension and calming restlessness.

Stress relieving moves in yoga combine moving and stationary poses paired with deep breathing, and when practiced regularly these moves cam also reinforce the relaxation response in the body. These moves serve as a type of mind body practice that combines gentle stretching exercises, controlled breathing and relaxation techniques.

Because an effective yoga session demands that the individual slows down and regulates their breathing patterns, all efforts are tuned on this intense concentration. This practice of fixation in a narrow sense, and meditation in a broader one is in itself a decompressing experience. When these are paired with certain asana, tension can be released from different parts of the body and symptoms of anxiety eased.

As the yogi shifts focus and attention to the body and breath, stress relieving moves will not only assist in tempering anxiety but also pacifying physical tension. The following yoga poses which are mentioned here may be practiced together or separately to facilitate relieving stress and anxiety in individuals. For some yogis closing their eyes while doing the moves may also help them relax and attain a more meditative state.

Seated Postures

Many of the seated postures in yoga will bring about feelings of calmness and put the mind in a meditative state.

Salutation Seal: This seated yoga pose is an ideal way to promote a state of meditative awareness. The move is performed sitting cross legged with both palms held together in the centre of the heart chakra where the practicing yogi will have their eyes closed. This position represents harmony and balance between the two sides of the body where both are reunited in the centre. This equilibrium symbolises not only physical balance but also the mental and emotional aspects as the idea is to centralize all focus on contemplation and meditation.

Easy Pose: Another seated posture, the Easy Pose requires the yogi to sit in a cross legged position with their hands resting on the knees with the palms facing up or down or alternately using a hand mudra.

The hip bone is pressed into the floor while the crown of the head is extended lengthening the spine. Shoulders are dropped down and back while the chest is pressed forward. This position is a comfortable seated pose that opens the hips, lengthens the spine and induces a sense of internal calm. To make the pose more comfortable, students may place a folded blanket under their knees or the hip bone. To get the maximum out of this pose, try to hold it for at least 60 seconds while focusing on the breath and sitting still with a straight spine.

Child's Pose: This calming position is a resting posture which can help quiet the mind, relieve stress and gently stretch the back. It is one of the fundamental poses that the yogi can revert to in the middle of a session whenever they want to alleviate stress.

To get into this position sit on the knees and bend forward with arms extended forward or alternately by the side. Rest forehead on the ground with the belly resting between the thighs. It is a gentle, stretching move that can stretch the hips, thighs and ankles while also relieving back pain.

Cat and Cow Pose: The Cat Pose helps soothe and stretch the lower back appeasing stress while at the same time massaging the spine. This position is often coupled with the Cow Pose where it involves deep inhaling and exhaling as the individual arches and rounds the back respectively.

These complementary moves are an easy and gentle way to warm up the spine and helps prevent back pain. The move also improves spinal flexibility and abdominal strength.

To get into the pose, start on all fours placing the hands underneath the shoulders and the knees underneath the hips. The spine should be neutral forming a straight line between the shoulders and hips.

On an inhale, drop the belly and take gaze up towards the ceiling. On the following exhale, round the spine and drop the head, taking the gaze to your tummy. Repeat the movement on each inhale and exhale moving the spine in coordination with each breath, after the final exhale, bring back spine to neutral.

Reclined Postures

Bridge Pose: The Bridge Pose provides a gentle stretch to the back and the legs relieving physical tension and mental stress. This pose can lessen anxiety, reduce fatigue, prevent backaches, headaches and insomnia and has even been considered beneficial for regulating high blood pressure.

A type of gentle backbend, the bridge pose demands the individual to lie on their back, and bend the knees while placing the feet flat on the floor hip width apart. At this point arms should be straightened pressing into the mat. Use this motion to gently lift the hips up towards the ceiling rolling the spine off the floor. Breathe and hold for 4-8 breaths. Slowly exhale and roll the spine back to the floor.

Beginners can try a restorative variation by placing a yoga block under the sacrum and letting weight rest on the prop.

Legs up the Wall Pose: Borrowed from restorative yoga, this move uses props to achieve a position that is a relaxing and gentle inversion. The benefits reaped from this move alleviate anxiety and stress, relieve tired or cramped feet and legs while gently stretching the hamstrings, feet and legs. The move can have a calming effect on the mind as it addresses a lot of the physical aspects of discomfort while providing mental relief.

The inverted yoga move is a gentle way to induce the body into a state of profound relaxation and recovery. A move that is often practiced at the end of yoga session, most typically before the Final Relaxation Pose or Corpse Pose, it can also be done on its own or when there is the need to relieve unwanted stress.

Legs up the wall can be done with or without props. Both variations cater identical benefits but the bolstered version may be more relaxed for participants.

Begin the pose by facing the wall in a seated position with knees bent into the chest. Gently bring lower back to the floor while raising legs up against the wall. Keep the body supported by elbows on the floor.

If using a prop, place the bolster or folded blankets against the wall first and shift the lower back onto the bolster before raising legs up. This will help increase the angle of inversion make the move more comfortable.

If the position is comfortable, hold it here for 5-10 minutes with eyes closed and breathing smooth.

To come out of position, bring knees into chest and roll to the side.

Corpse Pose: Most yoga sessions conclude with this simple relaxing move where the yogi is in position for several minutes before wrapping up a yoga class. The pose puts the entire body at ease and accentuates complete relaxation. Lying flat on the back with arms resting on the side, an individual's body triggers into a relaxation response where breathing is slowed, blood pressure lowered and the nervous system calmed.

Getting into the Corpse Pose pacifies the nervous system completely before it is forced to deal with the stresses of daily life. To get into position, lie down on back and allow feet to naturally fall out on each side. Place arms alongside the body but not touching it. Turn hands to face palms upwards. Let the whole body relax and breathe naturally. For complete unwinding, yogis are expected to stay in this pose for at least five minutes.

Standing Postures

Standing Forward Bend: This is a common yoga pose that is used as a transition between different positions. The forward bending motion provides a deep stretch as it stretches the hamstrings, thighs and hips. The stretch is helpful in relieving stress, minding fatigue and even combating mild depression.

To get the most out of this stretch, it is best done with knees slightly bent. Start from the Mountain Pose which is the foundation for all standing postures in yoga. From a standing position with feet hip width apart, hinge forward at the hips allowing knees to bend slightly so that palms touch the floor.

At this point there should be a stretch felt in the spine as the head is dropped down and the hips pressed up. Breathe and hold for 4-8 breaths and release returning to the mountain pose.

This posture helps lengthen the spinal column and stimulates a number of systems including the digestive, endocrine and nervous systems.

Where students feel it challenging to reach the floor with their fingers or palms, they can use a yoga block to make the move more accessible. A couple of variations on this move allow individuals to hold on to the back of the ankles during the bend, to cross arms behind the legs or clasp elbows behind the legs.

Triangle Pose: One of the foundational poses, the Triangle Pose is considered an effective stress reliever and provides a full body stretch to lengthen and open up various parts of the body. When done properly the benefits of this standing yoga position focuses on balance as well as energizing the body. The stretch also stimulates proper abdominal functioning while improving digestion and constipation.

To get into the triangle pose, start from the mountain position, placing feet comfortably wide apart. Turn out right toe to 90 degrees and the left foot to about 45 degrees. Turning slightly towards the right extend the torso and bend from the hip joint. Stretch right hand forward and rest on ankle. If reaching the ankle is challenging, rest the hand on the shin. Or alternately, on the floor next to the right foot.

Holding this position, stretch the left arm towards the ceiling aligning the hand with the top of the shoulder. Keep head in a neutral position and hold the pose for at least half a minute to one minute.

Reverse feet and repeat on other side.

For the beginner, the triangle pose is a great way to strengthen the core and the back. And because the pose also provides a gentle twist, it tests balance and flexibility of the spine.

Eagle Pose: Very different from the standing forward bend, which is a relaxing stretch, the Eagle Pose is a standing position that is an invigorating and empowering pose. This position is conducive in warding off stress because there is an immense amount of concentration and balance involved. With the yogi so directed on achieving this focus, tension is relieved through the shoulders, legs and back while all effort is centralised on maintaining balance. The eagle pose is considered an active de-stressing yoga move.

Getting into position requires that the yogi develops full focus, strength and composure by using breath and gaze to calm the mind and clear away all distractions.

Begin in Mountain Pose with arms at the side. Slightly bend knees and balance on one foot bringing the other to cross over your standing thigh. For instance if standing on the right leg, bring forward your left foot and cross over the right thigh. At this point, the gaze should be fixed on a single point in front of you. Now hook the top of the lifted foot being the calf of the standing leg. Balance.

Bring arms out in front and cross one arm over the other bringing the palms to touch. Lift elbows while sliding shoulders back. Hold for 5-10 breaths. Release and repeat on other side.

Because this move is so challenging, there are a number of variations available for beginners. For instance, beginner learners can forgo the foot hook and simply cross one leg over the other while resting the toes on the floor. Or they can place a block under the foot instead.

Likewise if it is too difficult to let palms touch each other after wrapping arms, then stop at pressing the back of the hands together instead.

To attain better balance, beginners can also practice the eagle pose while standing against a wall. Position the back against a wall so that it offers support when practicing the pose.

Chapter 9
<u>Yoga Poses for Weight Loss</u>

Effective weight loss can only happen when an individual's calorie intake is less than their caloric expenditure. In layman's terms a person needs to consume fewer calories than they burn in order to lose weight and keep it off.

Now the traditional way of losing weight is by engaging in strenuous aerobic activity while also participating in some sort of strength training. A combination of both these techniques helps achieve elevated heartrates that assist in burning calories while strength moves boost muscle build up. With more muscle and less fat on the body, weight is reduced effectively for prolonged periods and stamina is built up.

With yoga practices, on the other hand, weight loss should not be the only goal. Many types of yoga are sequences of gentle, flowing moves that cannot deliver long term weight loss in any case. Others that are more vigorous can provide a good starting point but hopefuls need to make sure that it is a session that is extremely challenging and can keep their heart rates elevated.

To lose weight, the type of yoga exercises incorporated in the workout need to be more than simply a mind experience accompanied by relaxing stretches, but should focus more on the physical aspect of the workout. Yoga types that are more of an exercise is what is needed in order to accomplish weight loss.

And while yoga is not a high intensity exercise by nature, there are some types like Vinyasa Yoga, Ashtanga Yoga and the more recent Power Yoga styles that can provide a fairly long session of cardiovascular activity accompanied by core work, balance postures and strength moves. To get sufficient weight loss results, individuals will need to engage in these energetic activity routines at least 4 to 5 times a week to get noticeable results.

As a benefit, however, including yoga in a weight loss routine can offer the advantage of revving up the metabolism. There are many yoga poses that have been known to boost metabolism which can in turn aid with better digestion and trigger a higher calorie burn.

But much more than the physical activity involved in doing yoga, the quality of yoga to foster focus and mindfulness in an individual will play a much bigger role in targeting weight loss goals successfully.

The awareness of how the body reacts to surrounding elements including food can trigger a shift in perspective. This self-awareness about an individual's relationship with eating habits can develop mindfulness about mealtimes, assisting in better perception about portion sizes, preparation techniques, as well as when to stop eating; when one is satisfied as opposed to eating until one is over full.

From this perspective yoga targets long term weight loss from a completely different vantage point. In lieu of restricting an individual's food intake as traditional dieting does, yoga nurtures the attitude instead. Rather than simply address the issue of excess fat on the body, yoga aims to focus on the triggers of overeating such as poor nutritional choices, emotional problems and other bad habits.

Because people eat for so many reasons outside of hunger such as when they celebrate, when they are depressed, or simply because others around them are eating, a long term practice of yoga can help resolve the problems of not how much or what we eat but those of why and how we eat. The more yoga is practiced, the clearer the awareness becomes of whether we eat out of habit or out of stress and sadness.

Through a sustained yoga practice, an individual can learn to change their body, improve metabolism and attain self-discipline. By increasing the awareness of the body, a yogi can recognize the ways in which to better take care of themselves by differentiating the true hunger signals from false ones and feed themselves what the body really needs.

To turn to yoga for weight loss, a few specific types will yield better results than others. Many of these more vigorous yoga styles demand stamina, strength, stability, and core work all paired up with a strong cardiovascular system. The poses all move relatively rapidly and will burn more calories than in a traditional, mind body yoga workout.

Vinyasa Yoga

Vinyasa Yoga is also known as flow yoga for the moves conducted in a session move from one posture into the other without any apparent breaks. Vinyasa is a more dynamic form of Hatha Yoga. The sessions use specific postures set to a choreographed routine where the poses do not end abruptly but glide into the next one in continuous motion.

Many of its moves are bodyweight exercises that are ideal for weight loss. By engaging in these poses continuously transcending from one to the next, all major muscle groups in the body are worked intensively. Within a Vinyasa Yoga session, a total body toning workout is achieved.

Vinyasa Yoga sessions are made up of a series of sun salutations that the yogi progresses through quickly raising the heartrate that is required for effective calorie burning leading to weight loss.

Ashtanga Yoga

Ashtanga Yoga is a style of yoga that involves fast paced poses that are sequenced together to provide a high energy workout session. The focal point of this type of yoga is extremely physical which includes a series of postures synchronised with various breathing techniques. The tempo at which Ashtanga Yoga moves are done heats the body's internal temperature and keeps it at an athletic pace.

When compared to other types of yoga, Ashtanga Yoga delivers an intense training workout that results in elevated heartrates and profuse sweating. Its benefits are designed to improve flexibility, enhance circulation and boost stamina while also building a lean and slim, yet strong body.

Given the intensity of Ashtanga Yoga moves, the program is not recommended for newcomers to yoga but for more seasoned practitioners.

Power Yoga

Power Yoga is a super active, fast paced sequence of flowing movements that are put together with meditative breathing techniques to achieve a strenuous cardio workout. Workouts are devised to provide effective muscular as well as cardiovascular benefits to participants while the meditative breathing helps to create harmony between the moves. Participants are pushed through the moves at a faster pace with less rest time in between. Along with providing cardio benefits to participants, Power Yoga also streamlines and aligns the body for better balance and flexibility.

This yoga style is very popular at health clubs and gyms and is attractive for health aficionados. The practice is built on the heat and intensity of Ashtanga Yoga and practiced with a fixed series of poses.

However, Power Yoga is not for everyone and individuals need to make sure that they are physically fit without any injuries in the back or knees. Additionally, they should not suffer from any breathing ailments or cardiovascular issues.

Hot yoga:

Similar to Vinyasa Yoga, Hot Yoga or Bikram Yoga also takes individuals through a series of poses. However, Bikram Yoga is always conducted in a heated studio where temperatures can go up to 105 degrees Fahrenheit. Moving through Bikram poses quickly allows participants to burn calories as well as lose water weight due to excess sweating.

Yoga Postures for Weight Loss

Deciding on the most suitable type of yoga for weight loss will depend on the individual's goals, fitness level and preference. However some of the most potent yoga moves for weight loss summarised below can offer to kick start metabolism and build lean, muscle tone.

Sun Salutations:

Sun salutations are an integral part of any Vinyasa style yoga session. In this sequence the breath is a very important component as moving from one pose to the next is always conjugated with either an inhale or an exhale. To commence the sequence the yogi needs to stand in the mountain pose with hands placed in the Anjali mudra.

With the first inhale raise arms above head in the Raised Arms Pose and hold. Exhale and release arms to the side and bend forward at the hips to go into a Forward Bend Pose. Inhale and come to a Flat Back Pose lifting head and flattening the spine. Exhale and return to Full Forward Bend once again.

From this position inhale and bring right foot to the back of the mat and come in a lunge pose on fingertips. Exhale. Inhale once again and bring left foot next to the right so that you ae now holding yourself in a Plank Position. The aim here is to form a straight line from the crown of the head to the heels of the feet without any drooping or sticking out.

Exhale and then drop to Knees, Chest and Chin Pose while keeping the butt lifted high and elbows hugging ribs. Inhale and move into a low Cobra Pose. Exhale and shift body into a Downward Facing Dog Pose. At this point stay in position a little longer if you need to take a breather or if aiming for a brisk pace, hold for on breath and move on.

Inhale and bring right foot forward next to the right hand, this position will bring you back into a Lunge Pose. Exhale and place the left foot next to the right moving into a Standing Forward Bend position.

Exhale and straighten into a standing position with hands in a prayer position at heart. Repeat the sequence on the other side.

Sun salutations are a great way to warm up before any yoga session.

Warrior Series: This series of moves target the entire body and can deliver an invigorating sequence of standing poses. There are five warrior positions progressing from the easiest at warrior I to the most challenging at warrior III and two intermediary positions in between.

To begin the sequence stand in Mountain Pose and take several deep breaths. This is a good way to lace the body in a neutral stance and focus on proper alignment.

Stepping back with the left foot to the rear end of the mat, come into Warrior I pose. Place left heel on floor and turn left foot to a 45 degree angle. At the same time slightly bend right knee over right ankle. Hips should stay in the same position as in Mountain Pose.

Inhale and bring arms over head, if possible press palms together but if too challenging, then keep hands raised at shoulder distance apart.

Release arms and bring them behind back clasping fingers together. With fingers interlaced and arms reaching back, bend forward at hips with head reaching for the floor. Hold position.

Rise and release arms stretching them sideways with the right arm coming forward and the left one going back to position for warrior II. The knee should still be bent deeply over the right ankle.

From this stance shift position into Reverse Warrior by raising right arm overhead and letting left arm slide down the left leg. The front knee stays deep as the raised arm take you into a backbend.

Release right arm and drop by side of the body. Pivot on ball of left foot and straighten right led from its bent position. Lift left foot from floor while hinging forward at the hips until the lifted left foot and upper body fall in a straight line parallel to the floor.

Arms may be straight by the side of the body or stretched in front of the body in line with the torso.

After holding the pose for the intended number of breaths, drop left foot and stand back up in mountain pose. Take deep breaths, regain alignment and repeat the sequence on the other side.

Cobra Pose: A move that works to firm the buttock and tone the abs, the Cobra Pose is suitable for all levels of yoga. To get into position, lie face down on the mat, with the tops of the feet flat against the floor. Pressing hips and legs down, place hands under shoulders, palms on floor and fingers spread apart.

Gently lift head, chest and then the upper back while pressing down on the hands. Keep gaze engaged forward and up at one point and elongate neck. Push back shoulders and experience the stretch through the length of the spine.

Bow Pose: This is an effective pose for toning muscle and losing extra fat from the arms and legs. To go into a bow pose, lie flat on the floor on your stomach. Lift legs upwards bending at the knees. Lift chest up stretching arms backwards and holding legs with hands. The move will cause the back to arch. Hold position and then release.

Extended Side Angle Pose: This pose is effective for targeting fat deposits on the side of the body. Stand with feet wide apart and turn right leg at a 90 degree angle. Keep left leg in stationary position. Facing forward, lower body to the right placing the right hand on the right thigh. Then lift the other hand up and stretch extensively towards the right side elongating the stretch over the head. Hold position and release. Repeat on other side.

For a more advanced version of the move, place right hand on the floor besides right foot or place on a yoga block for support.

Chapter 10

<u>Tips for Finding Inner Peace and Mindfulness</u>

Yoga is a soothing strategy that employs a number of techniques like kriyas, chanting and meditation to heal and cope with difficulties. But it is an art that one must learn and practice with precision to make it work. To gain inner peace, a yogi needs to let the mind control the body and not the other way around.

Since inner peace is a state of mind, it is something that can only be found within the individual or else emotions will be in control. When faced with turbulent situations, powerful emotions are triggered in many people. With emotions running so high, the natural inclination is to be impulsive and react excitedly. In addition, elevated emotions can easily carry an individual away and all perspective is lost for the moment.

Eventually this emotional flux leads to worry and anxiousness about how the situation might be righted again. Harassed by this continuous tumult, an individual easily loses their ability to think clearly and is unable to formulate an appropriate response in times of stress.

This is where a practice like yoga with its meditative aspect can come in handy for people who are looking for inner peace and mindfulness.

Yoga makes practitioners strong mentally so they can counter any situation serenely. Meditation helps recharge the mind and body so that there is more energy to do good things for the yogi themselves as well as for others around them. Through practice participants can learn to engage and redirect their thoughts, emotions, and energies into a positive channel.

A great analogy is to consider a session of mediation to be like taking a shower. When once having showered in the morning, an individual can then proceed with the remainder of their day without the need of repeated cleansing for the rest of the day. Likewise an early morning meditative session purges the mind permitting the individual to move ahead with other activities of life.

Yogic philosophy dictates that to attain a perfect state of health, the individual needs to remain calm mentally and be stable emotionally. In this philosophy health is not simply confined to the mind and body but also accounts for connection with the consciousness. To achieve this, yogic meditation advocates that the clearer the consciousness, the healthier the individual.

Meditative techniques can assist individuals to achieve inner peace by going through the following stages:

Calming the mind:

No doubt that preparing the mind to become still is the very first step. An unsettled mind that is exposed to unrestrained thoughts will naturally tax and drain out the energy called prana or the life force from an individual. This will leave people feeling fatigued, completely exhausted as well as frustrated. To counter this restlessness, many have turned to toga and meditation to calm the mind down comfortably.

In a calm state, the mind opens up to new possibilities and eventually greater wisdom.

Acquiring complete awareness:
Yogic meditation can help release stresses that burden the thoughts and mind, and leave it feeling refreshed and clear. Meditation is a practice that redirects the mind to the present moment and enables the individual to be completely attentive to the movement.

For yogis inner peace is a state of being mentally and spiritually at peace. To achieve this there needs to be sufficient knowledge and insight to keep the mind, body and spirit steady when faced with difficulties or distress.

De-stressing:
Meditation helps the mind and body in two simple ways- not only does it prevent stress from entering the system, it also assists in releasing stress that may have already accumulated there.

Stress is triggered when there are unanswered, unresolved and difficult situations that seem to neither have any apparent explanations nor any obvious solutions.

When yogis are able to filter this stress they are closer to stepping into a higher state of consciousness where they are no longer thrown off balance by harsh situations or frequent upheavals.

Plus, on an emotional front, meditation cleanses and nourishes from deep within and brings emotional steadiness into the equation.

Finding the answers:
In order to attain inner peace, it is important that practitioners are true not only to themselves, but also to others around them. It is imperative to know what is truly important and refine that truth. This gives individuals the perspective to view life through an honest lens and accept what is essential, what is superfluous and also what they have no control over; that is knowing what cannot be changed.

Once this truth has been accepted, the yogi can then develop a deeper and more meaningful connection with the mind, body and spirit. Meditation gives this chance to shed the excesses of the day and turn the focus inward; by regulating breath patterns and relieving tension from the body.

Meditating anywhere, anytime:

Meditation for inner peace is a practice that can be conducted anywhere anytime just to relieve the mind or simply to break away from the monotony of daily life. A suitable time to meditate is in the morning as it can provide the ideal opportunity to start off the day right with and clear and rejuvenated mind. The practice of early morning meditation can help individuals remain calm and composed all day.

A break from routine in the middle of the day can serve those well who find themselves stuck in a cycle at work. Meditation at such times can allow individuals to just be by themselves, disconnecting from the humdrum around and simply relaxing the mind to unwind.

With the acquisition of inner peace, the same is also reflected in external situations. This enhances emotional resilience reducing the likelihood of reaction and increasing the tendency of response. By every measure, meditation is an effective means to de stressing the mind.

Dealing with ailments through meditation:

And while many of the stressors of daily life can be triggered by external factors, there are situations when internal mechanisms cause individuals to feel weighted down. One of these is during times of sickness.

Illnesses in people can develop from a multitude of reasons like violation of natural law such as bingeing excessively and overeating. Likewise an illness may be imposed by nature such as an epidemic or contagion.

Now yogic philosophy advocates that nature itself will deliver a cure for these ailments since both health as well as illness are parts of the natural equation. By engaging in meditation, anxieties and stresses are eliminated which gives rise to a positive state of mind. Being in a positive state of mind has a similar effect on the body and hence the condition of the illness can also change.

How to experience a more meaningful meditative session:

A few tips on how to make the meditation session more substantial can decidedly make the experience more worthwhile. For starters, meditation can be made more meaningful and relevant by ensuring that the surroundings are comfortable. It is always recommended to meditate in a quiet place with minimal distraction so that the practice can be experienced deeply.

It is also recommended that practitioners meditate often and are regular with the practice. More frequent meditation will grant individuals the chance to observe its positive effects and benefits clearly.

And while meditation by itself may seem like sitting motionless in a fixed pose, it is recommended that individuals try some deep stretches before sitting down to meditate. Stretching is considered a preliminary step to meditation as it helps relax muscles, relieves tension from various parts of the body and makes for a more relaxed and enjoyable meditative session.

While meditating it is important not to restrict the flow of thoughts but let them continue uninterruptedly. In this way negativity will be filtered out leaving the individual feeling positive and refreshed.

The duration of a meditation session should at least span a minimum duration of 10-15 minutes. The yogi should not be in a hurry to open their eyes as discovering inner peace through yoga will deliver serenity by liberating the body, mind and spirit. Much of it can be achieved by a few quiet moments every day by dispelling internal negative feelings and making individuals more content as a being.

Chapter 11

Enhance Yoga with the Right Foods

Choosing to practice yoga is oftentimes an individual decision; whether it is for better health, for stress management, for meditative contemplation or any other reason, the impetus is innately personal.

Likewise complementing the practice of yoga with the right kinds of foods will also be unique to each individual. Like yoga, eating right can also be viewed as trying to achieve equilibrium and balance in life. It is a decidedly a personal activity that yogis will need to adapt to their body's requirements when trying to develop a mindful eating practice that can truly support and foster the practice of yoga.

However, like other dieting trends, choosing the right foods to enhance yoga does not come with a menu plan set in stone. Instead it is through a series of trial and error that yoga practitioners will come to discover foods that work better for them than others. The experience can both be eventful as well as challenging but finding the right blend of food choices will deliver long term weight loss results as well as improve the individual's overall health.

From a historical perspective, yogic eating principles are closely related to those of Ayurveda, the ancient Indian science of healing and preventive health. In Ayurveda, not all bodies are the same but are of varying types. This means that each type of body is affected differently by the type of food it consumes and thrives accordingly.

Knowing their body type or constitution known as prakriti can help an individual tailor a suitable diet plan which can assist them in acquiring a good balance between their mind body connections. Broadly speaking there are three basic body types which can be summarised as the following:

Vata: Those falling in this category are observed to be very active, mobile, even restless individuals. Such individuals are likely to have fast metabolism so are often thin structured with little muscle development.

Pitta: Individuals with a pitta disposition, often have a higher body temperature than others and tend to perspire excessively. These characteristics also make such people more emotionally expressive while also being more decisive, ambitious and aggressive.

Kapha: Those identifies as being kapha are often overweight, or have the tendency to gain weight easily and have a solid, large built. Such individuals display a moderate appetite and slow digestion. Activity levels are usually sluggish and lethargic in such individuals while they may be more prone to excessive sleeping habits.

So when deciding on the best types of foods to enhance yoga for each body type, these characteristics should be kept in mind. For instance, vata types are thought to need more grounding foods like oils and grains while pitta types can benefit more from consuming cooling foods like sweet fruits or fresh salads.

Kapha types, on the other hand are believed to profit by including invigorating foods like hot peppers and cayenne into their diet.

However, not every individual is exclusively a single body type but often displays characteristics of multiple types with one type being fairly dominant over the others. So a result it becomes important for all individuals to find the correct balance of foods to suit their own body constitution.

Just as specific yoga poses and postures are more fitting for different individuals, the same applies to different types of foods. A good diet for everyone, however, should aim at providing energy to the body and clarity to the mind. When individuals begin to experience strong digestion, good sleep quality, feel healthier and energized overall rather than depleted by their yoga sessions, they will have formulated their perfect diet for enhancing yoga.

Food Myths Surrounding Yoga

To help find a balanced approach to eating and one that supports yoga practice, it is equally important to debunk common myths that are highly prevalent in yoga communities. For instance, you may find yourself presented with the suggestion to go for hours without eating before a yoga session. Or you may be told never to engage in a yoga session for at least seven hours after eating.

Either scenario proposes an extended fasting period prior to a yoga workout that can actually be a debilitating experience rather than an invigorating one. And while it is true that overeating or eating just before a yoga session can seriously disrupt the workout by making the individual distracted or uncomfortable to fully go into the positions, not eating properly or worse, fasting before the yoga class will have a much more incapacitating effect.

Feeling devitalized due to lack of energy will only leave individuals feeling hypoglycemic, dehydrated and dizzy, unable to perform to their full potential in the upcoming yoga session. Here, the trick to avoid this unpleasantness involves being mindful and intelligent.

Just as during a positive yoga practice, participants are required to be aware and attentive, likewise they are also expected to be careful and cautious while approaching a yoga food practice and settle on an eating system that fulfills their physical, mental and emotional needs.

With continued yoga practice an intuitive sense of what is relevant and sufficient for the body will develop. Individuals will learn to identify foods that are satisfying and filling along with others that may cause discomfort or uneasiness. Experts recommend that observation and balance are instrumental in finding the right supportive foods.

Just as yoga postures teach individuals to align and coordinate the body, yogic awareness will also instruct practitioners to identify what types of food their body needs.

Food Choices in Yogic Philosophy

According to the five principles of yoga, following a yogic diet is one of them. The yogic diet philosophy does not take into account factors like calorie count but emphasizes instead on the type of food, its quality, and the effects it has on the body.

Choosing these foods to complement yoga practice will not only improve health but also contribute to detoxifying and feeling fitter.

Now traditional yogic discipline recommends a pure vegetarian diet which is based on the concept of avoiding any foods which involve killing or harming of animals. Known as a Sattvic diet, food choices are extracted from foods that are grown in harmony with nature.

But not everyone practicing yoga will want to become a vegetarian, so for a broader classification of dieting practices, dietary principles can be classified into the following three types:

Sattvic Diet:

This is the purest form of diet and the one most recommended for serious pursuers of yoga. It draws on sources of nutrition derived from nature. The diet nourishes the body and keeps it in a peaceful state. Foods in this diet calm and purify the mind permitting it to work to its full potential. Yogic philosophy dictates that including Sattvic foods into the diet leads to true health. It delivers a peaceful mind in charge of a fit body with a balanced flow of energy between the two.

Sattva is the quality of love, awareness and connection and is reflected in the dietary choices made by yoga enthusiasts. The foods in a Sattvic diet do not only come from nature but also need to be prepared with a feeling of love and connection for it is believed that foods prepared with love will enhance their Sattvic quality.

If they very same foods are prepared when the individual is upset or angry, these negative feelings will transfer into the cooking process and the meal prepared with lose its effectiveness.

Yoga basics prescribe that foods should be grown organically on fertile soil, they need to display a fresh appearance and be harvested at the right time of the year. These foods should be whole foods and be as close as possible to their natural state. Of course, this explanation goes to include that Sattvic foods are grown without the use of pesticides, chemical fertilizers, hormones or anything unnatural.

The food should be enjoyed for its natural taste and quality and not for the spices and seasonings that are added on.

Sattvic eating habits encourage eating in moderation while practicing a balanced diet. The yogic discipline recommends that only 50% of the stomach should be filled with food with another 25% filled with water. The remaining 25% of the stomach should be kept empty to aid proper digestion and maintain a healthy digestive tract.

Along with eating in moderation, it is also recommended to eat slowly while chewing the food properly.

Sattvic foods are light, soothing and easily digested. They include sun foods and ground foods meaning foods that draw their energy from the sun and the earth and provide excellent nutritional value.

This includes foods that grow close to the ground such as whole grains, and fresh fruits and vegetables. Whole wheat breads and pure fruit juices are by products derived from these. Some of the foods that form an integral part of a Sattvic diet include the following choices:

Fresh organic fruits:

Most fruits are considered especially Sattvic. In yogic disciplines fruit is symbolic of spirituality and generosity and functions as an appropriate offering or gift.

Fresh organic vegetables:

Most mild vegetables like carrots, celery, cucumber, and leafy greens are considered Sattvic. Others that are more pungent like garlic, onion and hot peppers are excluded, being classified Rajasic while yet others like mushrooms and potatoes are known to be Tamasic.

Fresh, organic dairy:

Dairy choices include milk, butter, whey, yogurt and cheese. When dairy is paired with fresh fruit, it makes for an important component of a Sattvic yogic diet.

Whole grains:

Whole grains like whole wheat, spelt, oatmeal, rice and barley are excellent examples. Grains may occasionally be lightly roasted to remove some of their heavy quality or grains may also be sprouted before cooking.

Legumes:

Bean sprouts, lentils and split peas are some examples. Legumes can be prepared by splitting, peeling, grinding, and sprouting. When legumes are prepared with whole grains, the meal offers excellent protein supplementation.

Nuts, seeds and oils:

Fresh nuts and seeds are useful additions in a Sattvic diet. However, caution should be exercised in using only small portions. Some good choices include almonds, walnuts, pine nuts, pumpkin seeds and flax seeds. Likewise oils should be cold pressed to yield the highest quality. Good examples are olive oil, flax oil and sesame oil.

To drink include herbal teas sweetened with honey. Honey is an all-natural sweetener that offers many natural healing properties as well.

Sattvic foods are fresh, nutritious and full of fiber and do not agitate the stomach.

However, just as Sattvic foods are highly recommended on a yoga diet there are other food groups and food types that should be avoided as they take away from the inner energy and sense of balance of individuals.

Among these the following two dieting trends should be eliminated or at least minimized to reap the full scale benefits of a yoga practice paired with good eating habits:

Rajasic Diet:

These are highly flavorful foods that are very hot, bitter, sour, dry or salty foods. Eating too much of these foods disrupts the mind body equilibrium by over stimulating the body. The practice of eating in a hurry is also reckoned Rajasic.

That being said, however, Rajasic foods do offer some yogic benefits. For instance, some Rajasic foods provide the kind of energy that is needed to accomplish, create and achieve. A combination of Sattvic and Rajasic foods is recommended for those who engage in demanding disciplines like endurance athletics, martial arts or other vigorous activities.

Rajasic foods include sharp spices and herbs, stimulants like coffee and tea along with food choices like fish, eggs, salt and chocolate.

Tamasic Diet:

This type of diet neither benefits the mind nor the body. Tamasic foods tend to be supplemented with too many spices, an excessive use of salt, artificial colors and preservatives. With Tamasic dietary habits individuals tend to lose their inner energy letting a state of inertia settle in. The body's immune system is compromised allowing disease to infiltrate more easily. In addition, Tamasic foods stimulate emotions of anger and greed.

Overeating is considered Tamasic and many people fall victim to various ailments due to habitual overeating or consuming the wrong types of foods. To continue eating even when beyond the scope of satiety reflects an imbalance in the mind body connection which is the driving force behind all yogic practices. Besides, overeating strains the digestive system making the body more sluggish.

Much of today's dietary patterns reflect a Tamasic way of eating. Fast food items that are highly processed and loaded with sugar, oils and preservatives offer very little nutritive value yet tax the digestive system heavily.

Tamasic foods include meat, alcohol, tobacco, onions, garlic, fermented and processed foods. Meats in particular are particularly questionable as they are injected with artificial hormones while alcohol and tobacco are known for their many detrimental effects on health.

Foods that have become stale and are no longer fresh are also classified as Tamasic foods.

Chapter 12
<u>What are Chakras?</u>

The Sanskrit word "chakra" is translated into English as "spinning wheel". According to yogic ideology these chakras are energy centres in the human body that are located along the spine. They start at the base of the spine and run upwards to the crown of the head. There are seven fundamental chakras, each of which radiates a distinct color as well as spiritual quality.

The colors of the seven chakras are taken from the spectrum with each hue denoting a specific quality. It is true that color can have a significant impact on individuals affecting their physical, emotional, mental as well as spiritual levels. For instance, sedate colors like blue, indigo and white generally have a calming effect on the eyes as well as the mind, whereas fiery colors like red, orange and yellow have a more invigorating and robust effect. For this reason, each chakra has also been assigned a particular color which governs that chakra and highlights its features. This detail to color and its meaning will be discussed a little later.

Likewise, the chakras are also linked with complementary physical, emotional and psychological states that are needed for the development of an individual.

This process of development allows individuals to mature in such a way that their life becomes more sublime, more stable and better connected to others. But since this change and maturity can only come from within, yogis believe in working with chakras to resolve any issues that may be preventing them from reaching their highest potential.

Based on yoga doctrine, there is a subtle part of the body that cannot be seen. It is in this understated mode of being where the body's energy flows. The seven chakras or vortexes of energy ensure that the energy flows freely but when some of it becomes trapped in a chakra, the result is physical, mental or emotional imbalance that can cause conditions like stress, inertia or even poor digestion in individuals. To deal with this unevenness in equilibrium, yogis can tap into the chakras as a way of mobilizing and redirecting energy in the direction that they want it to flow. Chakras are strategically placed in the body so that these energy centers are connected to major organs and glands that affect other body parts. On the physical level the proper functioning of the organs depends on the flow of energy within its chakra. So for instance, if the energy flow is disputed or blocked in any one of the chakras, then the corresponding part of the body will present symptoms of a physical ailment. Likewise, any imbalance in the chakra center will also impact the mental and emotional wellbeing of the individual.

Importance of Incorporating the Chakras

As centers of force, these seven chakras can be viewed as stations where life energies are received, absorbed as well as distributed. Based on the activity and influences of external situations, both stressors and stimulants, as well as internal habits, the chakra may become deficient or excessive, and consequently, imbalanced.

As a result of this disproportion, an individual may become afflicted with situational challenges that may be temporary, lingering or recurrent. When a chakra is deficient, it neither receives a smooth energy flow nor is able to spread it forward. The particular emotions and associations linked with the chakra get closed down with the individual displaying physical, mental and emotional symptoms.

Likewise when a chakra is excessive, there is an overload in its energy flow with the result that certain, physical, mental or emotional traits linked with the chakra become dominant in the individual, once again exhibiting disparities in character.

The triggers of these imbalances can be external factors like toxins, impurities, chemical enhancements in food and other environmental factors. These and other forms of pollution can cause instability in the chakra system which will manifest itself in the individual's health.

The importance of learning about the chakra system is that it gives insight into not only what is causing the imbalance but also provides solutions to correcting the equilibrium. Being aware of chakra functioning allows individuals to take better control of their lives in every aspect.

The vitality levels of chakras will indicate any apparent disturbances in its energy flow. Since each of the seven chakras has its unique function and intelligence, its performance can be detected from its energy flow. When individuals know about the elements each chakra is associated with, they can begin to figure out how that particular element perceives in the body.

When working with chakras, yoga poses will include postures that work to balance and promote the uninterrupted flow of energy though the chakra. A well-tuned asana session can help release trapped energy and stimulate an agitated chakra. The effects of a practice that incorporates chakra based moves can have an effective an empowering effect on the mind and body of an individual.

Chapter 13
<u>The Seven Chakras in Detail</u>

Each of the seven chakras is a discus of energy vibrating at a specific frequency. Starting at the base, as an individual moves up, the subsequent elements move from the physical to the subtle. For instance, the five physical elements of earth, water, fire, air and ether transition into the spiritual elements of light and cosmic energy. It is a logical and orderly sequence where the heaviest element is at the bottom and the lightest at the top.

<u>Root Chakra</u>

Natural Element: Earth
The first chakra is known as Muladhara or the root chakra. This center is located at the pelvic floor or the base of the spine. It is represented by the color red and a lotus with four petals.
The color red relates to a sense of self-awareness and provides energy on all levels. This energy is then spread to other parts of the body and carried out to the chakras above. Emanating from the ground, being the tap root, this chakra connects individuals to the Earth. The chakra keeps people grounded and close to reality, makes them physically strong and emotionally secure. The root chakra is also responsible for the instinctual urges centering on food, sleep, sex and survival.

So, naturally the root chakra is linked with those aspects of consciousness that represent security, survival and trust. In worldly terms, this translates into concerns with money, home and job. When the energy flow is smooth in this chakra, an individual will feel secure, shielded and well grounded. However, when there is a disruption in the energy flow of the root chakra, tension felt will be translated into fear or insecurity. When the same tension escalates further, it will be seen as a threat to survival.

On the physical plane, when the root chakra is out of alignment, it can trigger weight fluctuations, such as excessive weight gain or unexplained weight loss, anxiety, depression, pelvic pain or incontinence. On a mental front, disruptions in energy flow in the root chakra can cause individuals to be inattentive and restless causing anxiety, stress and exhaustion. On the other end of the spectrum, the same imbalances may trigger lethargy and the inability to take action in other individuals.

A positive balance in this energy center would translate into mental and physical health as well as prosperity. Individuals with a balanced root chakra feel strong and confident; feeling comfortable standing on their own two feet while taking care of themselves.

Balancing the root chakra is very important because it provides a solid foundation for opening the chakras above. Meditation can help with this process as, on the one hand, it connects individuals to an elevated spiritual plane, on another the practice also assists to ground them to the earth.

Some asana that can help open and balance the root chakra are the Mountain Pose, the Warrior I Pose, and the Standing Forward Bend Pose.

As mentioned previously, the Mountain Pose serves as a starting pose for many other asana and is an important one for grounding the feet and aligning the body.

Likewise, the Warrior I Pose is also a standing and grounding pose that stretches the arms and shoulders while strengthening the back and lower back. The Standing Forward Bend is another grounding move that stretches and relieves tension in the back while massaging and toning abdominal muscles.

Practicing these positions ground the root chakra while using the body's natural flow of energy to stimulate it. The poses connect the individual to the Earth giving them a strong foundation in the feet. With the root chakra located at the base of the spine, these moves gives the hips a nice stretch while releasing stale energy.

Sacral Chakra

Natural Element: Water

The second chakra called the sacral chakra or Svadishthana, is positioned in the sacrum, at the lower abdomen between the pubic bone and the navel. This chakra is symbolized by the color orange and a lotus with six petals.

Orange represents the sense of self-respect. The sacral chakra is the water center for people and holds their reproductive organs, and desires. When an individual's consciousness flows uninterrupted through this region, they can reach their potential for self-healing and sensual pleasure.

When working with this chakra, individual address their relationships with themselves as well as with others. With the sacral chakra out of alignment, individuals can experience chronic low back pain, urinary tract infections, ovarian cysts, and other reproductive issues. Additionally, there may also be complications with the kidneys and bladder.

Emotionally, the individual may feel guilty, unstable or self-critical, while the mental signs of interruption in the sacral chakra may be reflected as repressed emotions, addictions, and a lack of creative energy.

A positive balance in this chakra would result in stability in an individual's sexuality, sensuality and emotions.

The best sacral chakra moves are those that work the movement in the hips and the lower abdomen. Some yoga asana aim at opening the hips while others encourage energy flow through the region. Some poses to work on unblocking this chakra include the Cobra Pose, the Child Pose, the Twisting Triangle Pose and the Bound Angle Pose to name a few.

Working with the Cobra Pose reduces lower back tension, opens up the chest while building up strength in the shoulders and arms. This yoga posture boosts circulation allowing more blood to flow into the sacral area, stimulating the chakra.

The Child Pose stretches the hips, thighs and ankles in a gentle way and clams the brain. This moves allows energy to flow through the sacral chakra and awaken it.

The Twisting Triangle Pose helps move energy to the pelvic area while rooting the feet and balancing through the root chakra.

The Bound Angle Pose is a hip opener that shifts attention to the pelvic region where the chakra sits. Stretching the groin area helps release tension in the seat of the sacral chakra.

Navel Chakra

Natural Element: Fire

The third chakra known as Manipura is based at the navel, and is associated with the digestive system, the element of fire and individual purpose and power. The chakra is indicated by the color yellow and a triangle within a lotus with ten petals.

The color yellow is a creative and vibrant color which relates to the sense of self-worth. As such, the energy in this chakra is associated with the individual's self-esteem, personal identity, and individual will. This is the area where the personality, ego and intellect thrive and yellow lends clarity of thought and increased awareness to individuals.

The third chakra is considered to be the body's energy power house as it carries a lot of our physical vitality. On a physical plane, the third chakra is related to the metabolic and digestive systems.

When consciousness moves freely through this energy center, individuals are empowered, motivated, and confident.

However, when energy flow gets trapped here, and the chakra goes out of alignment, the resulting sensations may cause imbalances such as aggressive ambition, heightened ego and the pursuit of personal power.

On a physical level, digestive concerns can arise such as constipation and IBS due to improper processing of foods. Imbalances in this energy center can also translate into eating disorders, stomach ulcers, and other concerns with the liver, pancreas and colon.

Misalignment in the navel chakra will also impact individuals in their decision making powers. In some this imbalance can trigger aggressive, controlling or overly rigid behavior while others may find themselves giving in to a victim mentality, exhibiting a lack of self-esteem or direction. Feelings of low self-esteem, inertia and stagnancy will also prevail.

Successful alignment of the navel chakra will make practitioners more comfortable with their inherent power giving them a true sense of who they are.

Asana to open up the navel chakra include moves like the Boat Pose, the Warrior I Pose and the Sun Salutations.

The Boat Pose is an abdominal strengthener that stimulates this energy center causing it to open. In the case of an unbalanced chakra the Boat Pose reinforces strength as well as balance throughout the stomach region.

The Warrior I Pose is a heat building pose that also helps stimulates the navel chakra while the Sun Salutation Series also derive its name from the ability to warm up the core.

Heart Chakra

Natural element: Air

The heart chakra or Anahata, is placed at the center of the chest. This chakra is linked to the lungs and the element of air. The chakra is symbolized by the color green and a lotus with 12 petals.

The color green is a balancing color that relates to love and compassion, as well as the ability to give unconditionally. When well balanced, individuals are able to love, nourish and nurture themselves while relishing a sense of peace, harmony and renewal. Green has an appeasing effect that can help relax the body, and calm the mind.

When dealing with the heart chakra, the heart has the capacity to radiate the highest aspects of the being such as compassion, unconditional love and complete faith in the Divine. At the same time it also has the capacity to transmit the deepest feelings of loneliness, insecurity, despair and disappointment.

As such the heart chakra is correlated with those aspects of the consciousness that are linked to relationships and the perception of love. This can include an individual's affiliations with their parents, partners, siblings and children.

Given its central positioning in the body, this energy center also acts as a bridge between the lower and upper chakras integrating the visible with the invisible. Here the shift refers to a move from the physical to the spiritual. While some qualities of the physical world are associated with this chakra, the heart chakra is simultaneously linked with metaphysical features as well.

Because the heart chakra directly affects the heart, chest, lungs, arms and hands, any misalignment of energy here can cause cardiovascular complications, lung issues, poor circulation as well as high or low blood pressure.

On the mental level, an imbalanced heart chakra can trigger issues like manipulative behaviors, excessive possessiveness, co dependence, mistrust and feelings of unworthiness or fear of rejection.

Realigning energy flow on the other hand, will result in the individual feeling connected to everyone around while also experiencing love, compassion and joy completely. There would be sensitivity and unconditional love for all.

Asana and pranayama can be used to open up the heart chakra. Of these some examples are the Camel Pose, The Cobra Pose and Kapalabhati.

The Camel Pose stretches the front of the body, opening the chest and therefore also opening the heart chakra. Similarly, the Cobra Pose also enlarges the chest, and can stimulate the heart chakra.

Kapalabhati is a breathing technique used to specifically clear the chest and release any accumulated tension. The focus is more on chest breathing rather than abdominal breathing where inhalations and exhalations are short, rapid and strong.

Throat Chakra

Natural Element: Ether

The throat chakra also known as Vishuddha is associated with the element of ether. Vishuddha means very pure or purification. It is represented by the color blue and a crescent within a 16 petal lotus.

Blue relates to self-expression emphasizing speech, communication and expression. As such, this chakra is the energy hub of speech and hearing as well as of the endocrine glands that control metabolism.

The energy center is associated with the voice on a physical plane and relates to an individual's ability to speak the truth. It refers to the capacity to express ideas, clearly and truthfully. On a spiritual level, this chakra deals with the individual's capacity of expanding the conversation to the Divine.

It is also the first level of consciousness from where an individual can start to perceive beyond the physical and into another level of intelligent functioning. Ether serves as a crossover between the physical and the spiritual dimensions.

Physically the throat chakra is connected to the pituitary gland and responsible for growth and development. The chakra can be conceptualized as a spaciousness around the throat and neck through which profound spiritual truths can flow. When energy gets blocked in this region, a misaligned throat chakra may cause a sore throat, thyroid issues, neck and shoulder concerns, and other issues with hearing and jaw pain.

On a mental plane, trapped energy can cause the individual to suffer from an inability to express themselves coherently, with conflicting thoughts and poor communication.

However, when energy flow in this chakra is cleared and flows freely, it integrates the wisdom of both the heart and the mind as well. This results in spiritual truths to flow freely. An individual can then communicate their needs, desires, creative ideas, love and empathy effectively and effortlessly. Individuals experience greater intuition, inner knowledge and a feeling that they are much more than a physical being.

Some asana to work on the throat chakra include poses like the Fish Pose, the Camel Pose and the Plow Pose. The Fish Pose is a position that will open the chest and throat while relieving upper respiratory congestion. At the same time, muscles and glands in the throat area also stretched and opened stimulating the throat chakra.

The Camel Pose stretches the front of the body while applying pressure on the shoulders which stimulates the throat chakra. The Plow Pose works on clearing the throat from another angel. Typically, throat chakras are cleared by moves where the body is opened from the front. But with the Plow Pose the throat and heart are protected in the front while opening at the back.

Third Eye Chakra

Natural Element: Light
The third eye chakra known as Ajna is positioned at eye brow level mid brain. This is a crucial meeting point between two important energetic streams in the body where the mind and the body converge. The third eye chakra is represented by the color indigo blue and a lotus with 2 petals.

Indigo relates to self-responsibility and intuition. Energy from this color connects individuals to their unconscious selves strengthening instinct, insight and imagination.

Consequently, this chakra is associated with light where the third eye provides an access to a cosmic vision. In other words, this chakra is associated with higher knowledge where perception moves beyond the visual. Some can relate it to possessing extra sensory perception or ESP where inner senses correspond completely with outer senses. And the result is knowledge that is gained not through the physical senses but with those of the mind.

Also known as the sixth sense, it gives individuals an inner wisdom to face difficult situations. On the flip side, a misaligned chakra will result in feeling close minded, cynical, untrusting and too attached to logic.

Misalignment of the third eye chakra can cause problems with vision, headaches, migraines and dizziness. There may also be some mental confusion felt.

Individuals with a balanced sixth chakra will display a keen imagination, sharp intellect, strong intuition and a deep sense of spiritual awareness.

Asana to stimulate this chakra include The Child Pose, Eagle Pose and Trataka. The resting Child Pose is a gentle way to relieve stress and the forward bend connects the third eye to the ground, stimulates the third eye chakra or an individual's intuition. The Eagle Pose, on the other hand, is a more challenging asana that requires a lot of balancing. By concentrating heavily on maintain the pose, and keeping the gaze fixed on one point ahead, the third eye chakra is stimulated.

Trataka is a practice of staring at an external object where concentration is developed, eyes are strengthened and the third eye chakra stimulated.

Crown Chakra

Natural Element: Cosmic Energy

The seventh chakra is called the crown chakra or Sahasrara. It is epitomized by the color violet and exhibits the symbol of a lotus with a thousand petals.

Violet symbolizes spiritual awareness. Energy released through this color helps unify the individual with their higher self and higher consciousness. Violet energy enhances wisdom, purifies thoughts and brings guidance.

Hovering above the crown of the head this chakra links individuals to everything that is linked to the element of thought, connection to spirit, universal consciousness, wisdom, enlightenment and self-knowledge. It reflects everything that lies beyond the linear intellect of people as well as beyond personal needs, preferences and emotional experiences.

Just as the root chakra emphasizes a connection with the Earth, the crown chakra does the same with the Divine.

For yogis who work with this chakra, there is an interest in a greater purpose and an elevated way of being. These individuals are ready to let go of the physical and reach beyond the gateway and source point into enlightenment. The chakra addresses the issues of devotion, inspiration, spiritual understanding and selflessness.

Any complications in this chakra can lead to confusion, a lack of connection and an inability to function practically.

But an individual with a balanced seventh chakra would exhibit a greatly developed awareness reaching a higher spiritual state of bliss or even union with the Divine.

Asana to stimulate the crown chakra include moves like the Corpse Pose, the Half Lotus and the Headstand. The Corpse Pose in its lying still position challenges the individual to be connected to the ground while still being present in the moment. The horizontal position allows the crown chakra to open and let energy flow through all the other chakras.

The Lotus and Half Lotus positions are seated crown chakra poses that assist an individual to go inwards and connect with their inner wisdom and knowledge.

And the Headstand is an advanced pose that nourishes the crown chakra by drawing oxygenated blood to the head.

Printed in Great Britain
by Amazon